Asking the right questions about school
371.1°° °°° °°°°°°°°°°°°°°
Doug. T5-AET-919
FLETCHER FREE LIBRARY

Asking the Right Questions about Schools

A Parents' Guide

Chrys Dougherty

The Scarecrow Press, Inc.
A Scarecrow Education Book
Lanham, Maryland, and London
2002

SCARECROW PRESS, INC.
A Scarecrow Education Book

Published in the United States of America
by Scarecrow Press, Inc.
4720 Boston Way, Lanham, Maryland 20706
www.scarecroweducation.com

4 Pleydell Gardens, Folkestone
Kent CT20 2DN, England

Copyright © 2002 by Chrys Dougherty
Previously published by Omni Publishers as *Improving Your Child's Education: A Parent's Handbook for Working with Schools*, 1997, San Antonio, Texas.
ISBN: 1-891172-00-X

All rights reserved. No part of this publication may be reproduced, stored in a retrieval system, or transmitted in any form or by any means, electronic, mechanical, photocopying, recording, or otherwise, without the prior permission of the publisher.

British Library Cataloguing in Publication Information Available

Library of Congress Cataloging-in-Publication Data
Dougherty, John Chrysostom, 1951–
    Asking the right questions about schools : a parents' guide / Chrys Dougherty.
        p. cm. — (A Scarecrow education book)
    Includes bibliographical references (p.).
    ISBN 0-8108-4179-7 (pbk. : alk. paper)
        1. Education–Parent participation–United States–Handbooks, manuals, etc.
    2. Home and school–United States–Handbooks, manuals, etc. I. Title.
LB1048.5 .D63 2002
371.19'2–dc21   Library of Congress Control Number: 2001040425

∞™The paper used in this publication meets the minimum requirements of American National Standard for Information Sciences—Permanence of Paper for Printed Library Materials, ANSI/NISO Z39.48-1992.
Manufactured in the United States of America.

Contents

Preface

As a parent of two boys (now 10 and 14), I've had the good fortune to work with excellent teachers. And yet . . . in conversations with other parents, I've seen that many feel ill-informed about education. They are interested in knowing what questions to ask, how to evaluate the quality of their children's education, and how to become effectively involved. I also remember all of the things that I didn't know when my older son first started school.

I had been interested in education for a long time—since I helped a small group of community organizers start a child development program in Austin in 1972, taught science for several years beginning in 1974 in an elementary school started by the Black Panthers in Oakland, California, and wrote a report on federally-funded compensatory education for the House Education and Labor Committee in 1985. After receiving my PhD in Economics from Harvard in early 1992, I joined the faculty of the LBJ School of Public Affairs and worked on a state-funded research project in 1992 to develop an accountability system for the State of Texas. More recently I have become Director of Research of a nonprofit education data and research organization, Just for the Kids.

Yet all of this background did not fully prepare me to step into the role of an involved parent. Like most parents, I had to learn by doing. Fortunately, other parents, teachers, the school principal, and many others gave valuable advice. I decided that a book that blended this good advice with my own knowledge about education would be a useful tool for parents and the educators who work with them.

Acknowledgments

This book grew out of research, brainstorming, and chapter draft ideas developed by two year-long classes of graduate students at the Lyndon B. Johnson School of Public Affairs at the University of Texas at Austin. The following students made invaluable contributions to the research on the book:

In the 1994–95 Policy Research Project class: Cassandra Burke, Dwight Burns, Derrick Collins, Kim Cortez, Gwen Davis, Regina De Leonardis, Scott Harper, Shirlene Justice, Laura Lucinda, Andrea LaRue, Charis McGaughy, Dane McKaughan, Judith McFarlane, Carey Noland, Pat Samara, Drew Scheberle, Jennifer Unterberg, Christina Villareal, Sasha Wozniak, Kennard Wright.

In the 1995–96 Policy Research Project class: Kim Cortez, Helen Giraitis-Rodgers, Rebekah Hamilton, Penelope Kliegman, Cindy Leung, Sarah Lowry-Kihneman, Erin Mayton, Tracey Munza, Carey Noland, LaMarriol Smith, Brian Sullivan, Kristen Vassallo, and one student who perferred anonymity.

In addition, three students contributed draft paragraphs or pages that were incorporated directly with minor changes into the book: Helen Giraitis-Rodgers, Brian Sullivan, and Kim Cortez. Casis teacher Janice Mazzarella contributed invaluable research and drafts for chapter 2. Mrs. Mazzarella and Casis principal Amy Kinkade were extremely helpful in looking at the handbook through the eyes of educators who want parents to become contructively involved.

Generous financial support came from the Shell Oil Company Foundation, the LBJ School of Public Affairs Policy Research Institute, the James R. Dougherty, Jr. Foundation, Just for the Kids, the LBJ Family Foundation, Ben F. Vaughan IV and "Squeak" Payer, and Tom and Joanie Parr. Brad Duggan of Just for the Kids was instrumental in finding a publisher for the book. JFTK founder Tom Luce and LBJ School Dean Max Sherman provided strong encouragement along the way. Chula Sims provided assistance in identifying potential local donors.

The parents and teachers of the Hallsville Independent School District's Community of Learners project piloted the book and offered useful comments and suggestions. The pilot was arranged by Hallsville assistant superintendent Elizabeth Clark and consultant Alvis Bentley. Members of the board of the Appleseed Foundation donated copies of the book to Hallsville for the pilot.

In addition, the following educators provided comments for the book: teachers at Cedar Creek Elementary School in Eanes ISD; Eanes middle school principal Rick Bentley; Casis Elementary teachers Liz Eng and Carmen Scott; individuals in the curriculum division of the Round Rock ISD; and AISD Parent Involvement Coordinator Jo Ann Farrell. Parents and teachers from the Children's Advocacy Coalition and Barrington Elementary provided ideas on what parents need in a handbook. Alicia Hernandez-Sanchez ran the focus groups, while Lisa Hammel arranged for feedback from the Eanes and Round Rock school districts.

Helpful comments came from the following education experts: E.D. Hirsch, Bill Honig, George Farkas, Ethna Reid, and Phil Gough.

The following parents read the book and provided comments: Casis Elementary parents Anne Byars, Carla and Robert Dubois, Marcia Edwards, Yvonne Hellerstedt, Elizabeth Hummer, Kay and Gordon McNutt, and Pat Smith; O. Henry Middle School parent Debbie Hanna; Far Oaks Ranch Elementary PTO president Amy Brace; Live Oak Elementary parent Ginger Deegear; Dave Shearon; and Steve Klein.

Useful comments were also provided by Julian Shaddix and Bobbie Eddins of the Texas Association of Secondary School Principals, Sandi Borden of the Texas Elementary Principals and Supervisors Association, Randy Barrack, Roger Jones, and Janice Leslie of the Virginia Principals Association, and Dick Murray of the Ohio Principals Association.

Copyeditor Camille North provided invaluable assistance in helping me convert my academic writing style into something that more readable.

Finally, I would like to thank my wife, Mary Ann Krausse Dougherty, whose comments on the necessity of getting straight to the point contributed to the design of the book, and my two children John and Mark for providing an additional education in how children learn.

Introduction

Do you wonder whether your child is getting a first-rate education? Do you see many students getting As and Bs with little effort and wonder what those grades really mean? Do you see the same problems year after year in your local school district and want to know how to get involved?

Knowledge is power: the more you know about your children's schools and education, the better an education they are likely to receive. If parents in each school become better informed, then schools will improve. Why? Because those parents will encourage others to get involved and support teachers and administrators who want to make desirable changes.

This book will help you be an *informed partner* with your child's teacher. If you and the teacher work well together, your child will learn more.

HOW TO USE THIS BOOK

This book is divided into two parts. The first half is about being informed; the second half is about getting involved. Appendices in the back provide a glossary of educational words and phrases and sources of additional information.

This book does not need to be read straight through. Instead, read the chapters first that correspond to your own areas of interest:

- **If you have a child who may be in trouble academically,** begin with chapters 1 and 5.
- **If you have a child who needs to be challenged and you are interested in raising academic standards,** begin with chapters 1 and 6.
- **If you want to know what students in different grade levels should learn,** read the appropriate sections of chapter 2.

- **If you want to know more about the quality of your local schools,** begin with chapters 1, 3, and 4.
- **If you are worried about safety and discipline in your local schools,** begin with chapter 7.
- **If you are interested in the policies pursued by your school district,** begin with chapters 3 and 8–10.
- **If you want to get involved right away,** begin with chapter 11.
- **If you just want to be better informed,** read the book in several sittings and flag important ideas for later use.

THE BASIS FOR THIS BOOK

The book is motivated by the following ideas:

1. Parent involvement is extremely important in helping students learn.
2. Parent involvement is most effective when parents are *informed partners* with educators.
3. Ambitious but attainable academic goals inspire students, teachers, and parents.
4. Ambitious but attainable academic goals can build community support for a school or school district.

THE BOOK'S LANGUAGE AND CONTENT

Use of male and female pronouns. In order to recognize that teachers and students exist in both sexes, I alternated the use of pronouns by chapter: in odd-numbered chapters, students are "he" and educators are "she," while the reverse applies in even-numbered chapters. The alternatives were more awkward: using "he/she" and "his/her"; trying to make everyone plural; or using the male or female pronoun in all circumstances.

"First-rate" education in "good" schools. Use of these terms is designed to appeal to parents' aspirations for an excellent education for their children. Chapter 2 contains the author's view of what an excellent or first-rate education looks like, based on a review of the content standards listed in the notes in Chapter 2. Individuals and organizations with other views of what students should learn are urged to present these views to parents in order to encourage a healthy dialogue.

Research basis for the book. To prevent a clutter of footnotes in a popular book, I did not cite sources for every statement for which I have supporting documentation. Questions about the research basis for statements in the book should be addressed to the author at Just for the Kids, 301 Congress #575, Austin, Texas 78701, chrys@just4kids.org.

WHAT'S NOT IN THE BOOK

Because the book emphasizes educational *results* and not methods, you will not see much discussion of specific teaching methods—although a number of them are defined in appendix 1. If an educational method produces good results, then it is a good method; otherwise it is not.

In a similar spirit, we encourage you to focus on your child's learning results, *not* on the methods used by the teacher. You don't tell the employees in the local ice cream parlor, "Let me tell you how to make ice cream." Rather, you think *This had better be good ice cream.* If your child learns what he should in a safe and secure classroom, does the teaching method matter? If your child is *not* learning what he should, don't get sidetracked into a debate on teaching methods—work with the teacher on a plan to help your child improve.

Nor is this a book about child development or about helping your child adjust to school—many excellent books have already been written on these topics. We focus on schools' academic standards, how much your child is learning, and how you can work more effectively with teachers, principals, school counselors, other parents, and your own child.

YOU CAN MAKE A DIFFERENCE

A major theme of this book is accountability, which means *responsibility for results*. Though teachers and administrators are responsible for educational results, you bear the ultimate responsibility for your child's education and for the quality of your community's schools.

Our goal is to help you become better informed about the quality of your child's education and more aware of how to make a real difference. Read this book and get involved.

PART ONE

Learning about Schools

1

How Well Is Your Child Doing in School?

*When I became [my] child's stepmother, I was puzzled
and frustrated for some time by the dichotomy between
her achievements and her abilities. This "A" math student
asked her father and me just a year ago what the lines
meant on a ruler. She also was puzzled by fractions.
"Isn't ¼ bigger than ⅓," she asked, "since 4 is bigger
than 3?" This "A" history student had never heard of
the Holocaust, Prohibition, or the Salem Witch Trials.
Just a few weeks ago, she struggled to answer, "Who
was Thomas Jefferson?" only to finally reply: "Didn't he
invent electricity or the telephone?"*
        — *Parent of a suburban high-school student,*
                in a letter to the school principal

QUESTIONS ADDRESSED IN THIS CHAPTER

- Is my child learning enough?
- How should I interpret my child's grades?
- What do I need to know about grade inflation?
- How should I interpret my child's standardized test scores?
- How can I learn more from talking to and observing my child?
- How can I learn from teacher reports?
- How can I make the best use of teacher conferences?
- How can I work with the teacher if my child has a problem or
  needs extra attention?

If you are like most parents, you rely mainly on your child's grades to tell you how well he is doing. Yet an A in an easy course can mean little, and some schools give As and Bs to students who haven't learned much. To learn how your child is doing, look at *all* of the following types of information:

- grades
- standardized test scores
- reports by the teacher
- your own observations of your child's knowledge and skill
- his enthusiasm for learning

A problem in any one of these five areas may be compared
to a flashing red light: "Warning! Something may be wrong with
your child's education. You need to investigate."

Whether or not you suspect a problem, be alert! Keep a close watch on your child's learning, be aware of what students with a first-rate education are expected to know, and be constantly in touch with your child's teachers. When problems arise, discuss them with the teacher without laying blame.

IS MY CHILD LEARNING ENOUGH?

We want our children to learn at a level that is appropriate for their age or older, that challenges them, and that prepares them well for success after graduation. Here are some ways to find out if this is happening:

Find out your child's reading level. Ask the teacher. If your child can read and understand third-grade books but has trouble with books written for fourth-graders, then he is reading at a third-grade level. Many middle- and high-school students have trouble in school because they have poor reading skills. (See "What Is Your Child's Reading Level?" Also see chapter 5.)

WHAT IS YOUR CHILD'S READING LEVEL?

If your child is reading at a sixth-grade reading level, then he should be able to

- easily read books written for sixth-graders; ask your school's librarian for examples
- read books used in sixth grade in the schools where students learn the most
- score at or above the sixth-grade level on a standardized reading test

The teacher should assess your child's reading level in more than one way. Find out what assessments she uses.

Students who cannot easily read books written for their
grade are in grave danger of doing poorly in school.[1]

Ask your child's teacher to show you examples of satisfactory, good, and excellent work for his grade level in each subject. How does his work compare? Will he be doing excellent work by the end of the year? If not by then, when? What do you, the teacher, and he need to do to get him there?

Compare his current work with his earlier work. How much improvement is there? What new knowledge and skills has he gained?

Compare his work with work done in schools where students learn the most. Visit the best public or private schools you can find and look at samples of the students' work on display. If your child is an "average" student, compare his work with that of average students as well as the best students.

What you are looking for is *not* differences in teaching methods or the order in which things are taught—these are up to the teachers—but in how high the standards are. Are their students expected to do higher quality work? Are they learning more at an earlier age?

See chapter 4 for ideas on how to identify
schools where students learn the most.

Consult a challenging curriculum to find out what your child should learn. Ask teachers in the best schools to give you a written description of what their students are expected to learn (see chapter 2).

See if he finds his work interesting and challenging. Is he continuously introduced to new material and complex ideas? Is he encouraged to think? Is he inspired to move ahead?

> If your child is bored with school, that may be a
> sign that he isn't being challenged (see chapter 6).

See if your middle- or high-schooler is taking advanced courses. Does his school encourage him to take these courses? If not, why not? (See "Is Your Child Taking Advanced Courses?")

> Your child should take advanced courses even if he doesn't
> currently plan to attend college. He may need help
> catching up before he can take these courses (see chapter 5).

IS YOUR CHILD TAKING ADVANCED COURSES?

How do you tell if a course is advanced? Schools often identify courses as advanced by labeling them as "honors" or "college preparatory." Unfortunately, some of these courses don't live up to their labels. How can you tell the difference? The course should

- Challenge your child with difficult material. He should have to work hard to do well in the course. He should be expected to write, do research projects, and solve challenging problems.
- Impress you and him with how much there is to learn.
- Encourage him to think about the importance of what he is learning. He should be able to explain why the knowledge is valuable to people outside of school and how it relates to other things he has learned.

- Enable him to do well on Advanced Placement (AP) tests. These exams, offered in high school, give students credit for college-level work. Find out how many students who take the course later take and pass an Advanced Placement test in the same subject (not all courses lead to AP tests). The school's principal should have this information.[2]

Look at what standardized tests say about his strengths and weaknesses. Does this match your own observations and the reports from the teacher? Does the test highlight strengths or weaknesses that you had overlooked?

Show samples of his work to teachers in higher grade levels and ask whether he is well prepared. Talk to middle-school teachers if your child is in elementary school, high-school teachers if he is in middle school, or college professors if he is in high school. Get opinions from teachers in advanced or honors classes as well as regular classes.

Take a sample of your high-schooler's work to a local employer who pays high wages and ask the managers if he is being prepared for employment. Find out if A-level work by the school's standard represents high-quality work by the employer's standard.

HOW SHOULD I INTERPRET MY CHILD'S GRADES?

Grades usually reflect how well your child is doing in the opinion of the teacher or in relation to the school's standards. If these standards are too low, the result is grade inflation—students receive easy As and Bs but don't learn enough (see chapter 2 on standards). To find out what the grades in your child's classroom or school mean:

Ask the teacher what her standards are for A-level work. This may differ from teacher to teacher. Is A the same as "excellent"? What do students have to know and do to earn an A? Ask her to show you samples of A and B work and explain the differences between them.

Find out whether she takes effort and improvement into account in assigning grades. When achievement, effort, and improvement are combined into a single grade, it's hard to tell what the grade means. She should give you separate information about your child's performance level, improvement, and level of effort.

> Sometimes grades are used to reward good behavior.
> Well-behaved children may receive good grades even
> when they are having academic difficulty.

Find out the rules for grading late or incomplete assignments. Also find out how the school converts number grades to letter grades and if the school has clear standards for satisfactory and unsatisfactory work.

Find out how the A students in the school do on district-wide or statewide standardized tests. You can also compare the number of students who score high with the number of A students in the school. If many A students did poorly, that casts doubt on whether the grades mean that the students are well prepared. (Your school's principal has access to this information. See chapter 3 on assessments.)

> The teacher or principal may not be accustomed to parents'
> asking for this information. Work with the teacher, principal,
> and school board as they learn that parents want to
> be better informed (see chapters 4 and 11).

Find out whether the teacher "grades on the curve," that is, based on students' *relative* performances—the top students earn As, the next students earn Bs, and so on, no matter what their actual scores. Under this system, if a student's performance remains the same while his classmates do worse, then his grades will improve. This may create an incentive for him to pressure his peers not to study (see chapter 9).

WHAT DO I NEED TO KNOW ABOUT GRADE INFLATION?

Grade inflation is widespread. More than 80 percent of the 1.1 million students who took the College Board exams in 1990 reported a B or better grade average. Yet 40 percent of those students scored below 390 on the verbal part of the test, indicating that they were poorly prepared for college-level work.[3] (See "How Can You Spot Grade Inflation?")

Well-meaning parents and administrators often put pressure on teachers to inflate grades. Some parents want their high-schoolers to receive As so that they can get into good colleges, while some administrators believe that good grades build good feelings among parents and motivate students.[4]

Grade inflation is encouraged by the belief that education is a credential-getting game, not a learning activity. If the goal is to give the students a diploma and a good grade point average at minimum cost, then why not give everyone an easy A?

A mathematics professor, Andrei Toom, describes what happens when students think this way:

> [The students'] first priority was to get papers that certify that they are competent rather than to develop real competence....They seem to think that they *buy* grades and *pay* for them by learning. And they try to pay as little as possible! ... After every test I explained correct solutions. Many a student said: "Now I understand." I was glad: The purpose of my teaching was achieved. But some said it with regret, which meant: "This understanding is useless because it came too late to provide me a good grade."[5]

Grade inflation may be one reason why many parents of poorly educated students believe their children are doing well. Four out of five public-school parents think their children are being well prepared for high school, and two out of three think they're being well prepared for college. Yet 73 percent of American eighth-graders cannot consistently solve problems involving fractions, decimals, percents, and simple algebra.[6]

Grade inflation is worse in high-poverty schools. One nation-wide study found that A students in high-poverty high schools had scores on a standardized math test similar to those of D students in middle-class areas.[7]

HOW CAN YOU SPOT GRADE INFLATION?

The following signs may mean that grade inflation is a problem in your child's school:

- Many students get As even though their work doesn't seem to be of high quality.
- Many A students do poorly on standardized tests. Few of the high school's A students can pass Advanced Placement tests or other challenging outside exams.
- Many A students are poorly prepared for the next level of education. For example, many of the high school's A students must take remedial courses when they get to college.

If grade inflation is a problem at your school, pay extra attention to other measures of your child's success, such as standardized test scores, comparisons of his work with samples of excellent work, and your own observations that he is mastering a challenging curriculum, such as the one described in chapter 2.

> Don't encourage grade inflation! Demonstrate your own commitment to high standards. Don't ask teachers to give your children grades or promotions they haven't earned. The goal is a good education, not just a good report card.

HOW SHOULD I INTERPRET MY CHILD'S STANDARDIZED TEST SCORES?

A standardized test is any test given and scored the same way in different classrooms and schools. Some tests compare how your child does relative to students in other parts of the country, while others tell whether he has mastered a certain body of knowledge or set of skills. (See "How to Interpret Your Child's Standardized Test Scores.")

Find out what parts of the test your child scored the highest on and where he had the most difficulty. The school should provide a report on how he did on each section of the test and give you a clear and detailed explanation of the skills tested. Some school districts allow you to see his completed test—if so, review his mistakes.[8]

If he did poorly on one or more sections of the test, try to figure out why. He may have had a bad day, failed to follow directions, been nervous, or simply not "tested well." However, there may be real weaknesses in his academic skills.

See if the test reveals the same pattern of strong and weak areas as do grades and teacher reports. Does the test show something that you and the teacher previously overlooked?

Look for your child's improvement over time. What is his percentile rank, grade equivalent, or percentage of skills mastered this year, relative to last year?

Take note of his reading level if this is reported.

Remember that tests don't measure what your child is capable of learning in the future, only what he has learned so far.[9]

HOW TO INTERPRET YOUR CHILD'S STANDARDIZED TEST SCORES

Standardized tests are of two basic types:

- Norm-referenced tests compare your child's performance with a comparison group of students—usually intended to represent students nationwide.
- Criterion-referenced tests report whether he did well enough to pass each section of the test. (Passing may or may not imply mastery of the subject.)

Both norm- and criterion-referenced tests report *the number and percentage of questions he got right.*

Your child's percentile rank is different from percent correct: percentile rank is *the percentage of students in the comparison group who did worse than your child.* Even if he got only 40 percent of the answers right, but 90 percent of the comparison group students did worse, he would score at the ninetieth percentile.

A grade equivalent of 7.3 on a fifth-grade test does not mean that your fifth-grader has mastered seventh-grade material. Instead, it tells you that he did as well as a typical seventh-grader would be expected to do on the same fifth-grade test. The ".3" means that your child did as well as the typical seventh-grader who had been in school for three months. To tell if your child has mastered seventh-grade material, he would need to take a seventh-grade test.

HOW CAN I LEARN MORE FROM TALKING TO AND OBSERVING MY CHILD?

Talk to your child about what happened that day in school and what he learned. His answer may be "Nothing." Here are some possible conversation starters:

What did the teacher expect you to learn today? What did she talk about? Was she easy to understand? Was this material you already knew?

- What will you study tomorrow?
- What was the best thing that happened to you today? What was the worst thing?
- Did you learn anything from something you did? Did you learn anything from what someone else did?

See if he understands the educational purpose of each assignment. See if you understand it, too. If neither of you understands it, contact the teacher to find out how the assignment fits into the school's curriculum.

Observe any difficulty he has completing homework assignments. "I can't" may be his way of saying, "I don't feel like doing this." If your child has trouble getting started, ask him what he needs to do first, what he needs to do next, and so on. Are there important skills for completing the assignment that he doesn't have? Always look over his homework, but don't do it for him (see chapter 11).

Get a copy of the school's curriculum. This is the description of what students are expected to learn. See how many of those things your child appears to know. Pick a few items or skills and see if he, playing "teacher," can explain or demonstrate them to you (see chapter 2).

> Show enthusiasm for your child's learning
> and for learning new things yourself.

HOW CAN I LEARN FROM TEACHER REPORTS?

Read all of the information the teacher sends you! You should receive information on what your child has learned, what he is expected to learn by the end of the year, and how you can help (See "Five Kinds of Information Your School Should Provide"). If you're not getting this information, contact the teacher. If she sends you something you don't understand, have her explain what it means (See "Keep Track of Your Child's School Information"). The teacher may send you information in several forms:

- Skills checklists provide information about what your child knows and what he has just learned. Make sure you understand what every item on the checklist means. Pick two or three skills and ask the teacher how she judges whether your child has mastered each one. Does she apply that same standard for every child?
- Teacher comments should describe your child's strengths and weaknesses and what to do about them: "Johnny likes to read, but he still has difficulty reading third-grade books. Read to him at home as much as you can, and take turns reading from some of these books. . . ." Such comments as "Johnny is a great kid," though appreciated, are less informative.

- Folders and collections of your child's work can let you see what he's learning. Some schools keep samples of his work for every year since he entered the school—ask to look at them. Talk to the teacher if you have questions about this work.
- Scores on schoolwide tests may tell about his performance. Some of these tests may be designed by the school itself.
- Teacher newsletters can report on what the class has done and is planning to do and what the students are expected to learn.
- Report cards often contain a mix of grades, skills checklists, and teacher comments. Make sure you understand everything that is on the report card—if not, ask the teacher.

KEEP TRACK OF YOUR CHILD'S SCHOOL INFORMATION

Avoid big surprises by keeping important information about your child:

School communication folder: Include the school calendar, announcements, descriptions of school policies, and letters you write to school officials and their responses.

Teacher communication folder: Include teacher newsletters, notes from the teacher, notes from teacher conferences, and letters you write to the teacher and her responses.

Academic progress folder: Include copies of your child's report card and test score reports. In addition, you may want to make a folder for each grade and academic subject containing a sample of his work from each month.

Recognition folder: Include all special awards that your child receives—for example, science fair or art show ribbons or spelling bee finalist certificates.

FIVE KINDS OF INFORMATION YOUR SCHOOL SHOULD PROVIDE

1. Information on what your child is expected to learn in each academic subject. This should be written in language you can understand.

2. Information on the school's standards for excellent work. What are the standards for excellent writing or performance in mathematics? How do these compare to the standards used in other schools?
3. Information on what your child has learned in each subject. Is he making adequate progress? Does he consistently do excellent work? If not, how can you, the teacher, and he work together to get him up to that level?
4. Information on the school's success in educating all of the students. Your child is affected by how well his schoolmates are doing. How many of them are reading as well as they should? How many are weak in writing, math, history, geography, or science, and what is being done to catch up the ones who are behind? Where have students been successful, and what can we learn from their successes?
5. Information on how you can help. What can you do at home to help your child learn? How can you volunteer at school?

HOW CAN I MAKE THE BEST USE OF TEACHER CONFERENCES?

There are three important things to know about teacher conferences:

The appointment with your child's teacher can be as important as the appointment with his doctor. Many children run as great a risk of being set back by educational deficiency as by illness. If you simply can't get away from work during the usual conference time, make an appointment for a different time.

There is no way to discuss everything you need to talk about in thirty minutes, twice a year. Make the teacher conferences part of a series of conversations you have with the teacher. If you can't make it to the school easily, then contact the teacher periodically. Find out from the teacher the best times to call.

It's important to continue talking with teachers as your child goes through middle and high school. Parent involvement usually drops off in those grades and it shows—an alarming number of high-school students do not take their education seriously.[10]

Here are some tips for a successful conference:

Decide in advance what you want to talk about. What do you want to know about your child's academic progress, work habits, behavior, and social skills? What do you want the teacher to know about him? If the teacher has scheduled a three-way conference with your child present, talk to the teacher ahead of time to find out what will happen at the conference. Will your child do a presentation, answer questions posed by you and the teacher, or discuss samples of his work? What share of the talking should you, the teacher, and the child expect to do?

> Mentioning ahead of time items to be discussed will help the teacher prepare for the conference more effectively.

Allow at least thirty minutes for the conference. This gives you and the teacher time to have a good conversation about your child. The school can help by giving teachers more conference time.

Focus on only one or two major issues that can be addressed in a reasonable length of time. When several issues need to be discussed, schedule other meetings or conversations with the teacher.

Begin the conference on a positive note! Tell the teacher what your child likes about the class or teacher, and one or two things she's doing that you greatly appreciate.

Get past the "Johnny is a great kid who is doing very well" conversation. Discuss specifically what he is expected to learn, what he most needs to work on, and what you can do at home to help (See "Questions to Ask at Your Teacher Conference").

TYPES OF QUESTIONS TO ASK
AT YOUR TEACHER CONFERENCE

What are my child's greatest strengths? Greatest weaknesses?

- What is his reading level? How is it measured? How often is it measured?

- What has he learned in math, history, and science in the last six weeks? What will he be learning in the next six weeks?
- Can you show me how his writing has progressed since the beginning of the year? What does he need to work on the most?
- Can you show me examples of excellent, good, and satisfactory writing? Where does my child's work fit into this picture?
- Does my child work hard and finish his work on time? Does he revise his work to make it neat and use correct grammar and spelling?
- What is your policy on assigning homework, and how much time should my child spend on it each night?
- What is he doing in art, music, and drama? How can I develop his skills and talents in these areas?

Ask the teacher to show you samples of your child's work. You should be able to compare recent work samples with those taken from earlier in the year.

Tell the teacher anything she needs to know to work effectively with your child. As a parent, you know his personality and circumstances better than his teacher does. If there has been a major change or upset in his life, let the teacher know about it.

> Let the teacher know that you want your child's grades to be a true reflection of the quality of his work and that you understand that grades are only *one* aspect of school success.

Concentrate on your child's learning *results*, not the methods used by the teacher. How well he can read is a result; whether his teacher uses a "phonics-based" or "whole language-based" reading program is a method. Different teachers may use different methods to get results, and some teachers use a variety of methods to reach different children. (See "Teaching Methods and Educational Results: What's the Difference?")

Set a date to follow up on what was discussed at the conference. You should write down things that you and the teacher discussed, suggestions that she made, and any plans that you made to follow up on what was said.

TEACHING METHODS AND EDUCATIONAL RESULTS: WHAT'S THE DIFFERENCE?

In general, *educational results* are your child's knowledge and skill. Questions about results include

- Does my kindergarten child know the letter names and sounds?
- How well can my child read?
- How well can he write?
- How well can he spell?
- Does he know the multiplication table?

Teaching methods are what the teacher does in the classroom to produce these results. Does she teach letter sounds by having the students fill out worksheets, trace letter shapes in the air while saying the sounds, or bake cookies in the shape of alphabet letters and discuss the sounds the letters make? Does she have the students write every day? Do they take a spelling test every Friday? Do they play multiplication games and fill out practice worksheets with multiplication problems?

> Don't get sidetracked into a debate with the teacher about educational philosophies or teaching methods. Stick to what your child can and can't do and work with his teacher on a plan to help him learn what he doesn't know.

HOW CAN I WORK WITH THE TEACHER IF MY CHILD HAS A PROBLEM OR NEEDS EXTRA ATTENTION?

If you're reading this before something has gone wrong, don't wait until there's a problem to get to know your child's teacher. Also, see chapter 5 on preventing academic failure.

Meet with the teacher to discuss the problem. (See "Tips for a Teacher Conference When Your Child Is Having Trouble.")

If the issue is your child's academic skills, ask the teacher to develop a plan to improve those skills. Find out what you should do in the home to help out, and then do it consistently! Just as you should make sure he takes his medicine when he is sick, it is your responsibility to make sure he follows the teacher's "prescription."

> Behavior problems may be a sign that your
> child is having academic difficulty.

Find out about local tutoring and other academic assistance programs (see chapter 5).

When the issue is your child's work habits or behavior, work out a plan with the teacher or counselor to help him. Remember that he may not act the same way at school as he does at home. Have the teacher mention specific examples of the behavior, and ask how frequently the behavior occurs. Find out how you can support the teacher in her efforts to improve his behavior and work habits.

Schedule a follow-up meeting with the teacher to discuss his progress and see how well your joint plan is working. Let the teacher and counselor know how much you appreciate their concern and interest.

> Don't wait until there is a problem to get to know
> your child's teacher! See chapter 11 for more on working
> with your child's school and helping him at home.

TIPS FOR A TEACHER CONFERENCE
WHEN YOUR CHILD IS HAVING TROUBLE

Ideally, the teacher will call you and set up a conference as soon as she sees that your child is experiencing difficulty. If you think that he has a problem, however, don't wait—call the teacher and set up a meeting. During the conference, you should expect the teacher to

- Give you a brief overview of your child's progress. She will begin by telling you about the areas in which he is experiencing success. Then she will tell you about her concerns.
- Describe the difficulty he is experiencing and show you examples of his work. She will describe what he is expected to do and where his work did not meet the expectations for his grade level.
- Compare his work with the school's standard for excellent, good, and satisfactory work in order to show the progress he must make to produce excellent work.
- Describe what you and he must do to improve his work. She will discuss what she is doing in the classroom to help him.

If the problem is behavioral, the teacher will give specific examples of his behavior and work with you on a plan to help him improve.

**CHECKLIST: KEEP TRACK OF YOUR
CHILD'S ACADEMIC PROGRESS**

☐ Find out what the standards are at your child's school. Ask the teacher to show you samples of satisfactory, good, and excellent work and how they were evaluated. How do these standards compare with those in the best schools?

☐ Learn what your child's grades mean. Does an A mean that he is consistently doing excellent work? Do you receive separate information on his knowledge/skill, improvement, and level of effort?

☐ Know his reading level. See if he can easily read and understand books written for his grade level. Can he also read more advanced material? Does he enjoy doing so?

☐ Look at his rate of improvement. Compare his current work to his earlier work. At this rate of improvement, will he be doing excellent work next year?

☐ Observe whether he is continuously challenged. Are new materials and complex ideas presented throughout the school year?

☐ Look at what standardized tests reveal about what he has learned. What are his strengths? In what areas does he need to improve?

☐ Read all information his teacher sends to you. Call the teacher if you do not regularly receive information or if you have any questions. Make folders with reports from the school, samples of his work in each subject, and his awards.

☐ Show examples of his work to teachers in higher grade levels or to employers. Find out whether they think he is prepared to do well in their classes or in the workforce.

☐ Find out which courses are advanced. Enroll your child in them. If he doesn't have a strong enough academic background to take advanced courses, find out how to get him ready.

☐ Schedule two or three parent teacher conferences per year. Contact the teacher periodically to discuss your child's progress.

☐ Work with the teacher and counselor to develop action plans if problems arise.

CHECKLIST: PARENT-CHILD COMMUNICATION

What You Need to Do	Done	Follow-up
Get a copy of the school's curriculum and review your child's work. See what skills and knowledge he has attained. Play school with him as the teacher! (Source: teacher, principal, or district)	☐	Contact the teacher whenever your child seems to experience any difficulty.
Keep track of his homework assignments. Does he have difficulty with the work, and is it complete and of high quality?	☐	Call the teacher if he does not bring home any homework.
Ask him what he thinks he is learning from a particular assignment. Make sure its purpose is clear to both of you.	☐	Call the teacher if assignments are frequently unclear to you and your child.
Ask him about what happened in school each day. What did he enjoy or dislike, and what did he learn?	☐	I know what my child did in school today. I know what his favorite subject is. We spend time together on activities other than watching television.
Observe how he behaves. What topics does he avoid; does he seem happy or unhappy; does he seem eager to go to school each day; or does he find excuses to be late or absent?	☐	Contact your teacher if he is not enthusiastic about learning or wants to avoid school.

CHECKLIST: PARENT-TEACHER CONFERENCE

Schedule two or three conferences a year with each of your child's teachers.

Before the conference
1. Ask your child what he wants you to discuss with the teacher.
2. Write down your specific questions and concerns.
3. Decide on one or two major issues you want to discuss.
4. Let the teacher know in advance what you want to discuss.
5. Bring your parent-teacher communications folder and academic progress folder.

During the conference
1. Begin the conference on a positive note! Tell the teacher what kind of progress you've noticed and what your child enjoys, and thank her for meeting with you.
2. Ask the teacher to show you samples of satisfactory, good, and excellent work; to tell you how this work was evaluated; and to explain how a specific example of your child's work compares.
3. Focus on specific performance (not teaching methods), your expectations, and what you can do to help your teacher provide the best educational experience for your child.
4. Be sure to get past "great kid" comments to discuss your child's specific strengths and weaknesses.
5. Write down any plans or activities you develop together to improve your child's academic performance or behavior.
6. Restate important points the teacher makes to be sure you avoid misunderstandings.
7. You may not always agree with the teacher—respectfully tell her when you do not and let her know you will continue to explore the issue further with her.
8. Schedule a follow-up visit, if necessary, or let the teacher know you will keep in contact by phone.

After the conference

1. Write a thank you note and restate any important remaining concerns.
2. Contact the teacher when you need more information on your child's academic progress.
3. Discuss the conference with your child so he knows what you've learned and how you plan to work together with the teacher.

NOTES

1. See Dee N. Lloyd, "Prediction of School Failure from Third-Grade Data," *Educational and Psychological Measurement* 38 (Winter 1978): 1193–200; and Philip E. Kraus, *Yesterday's Children: A Longitudinal Study of Children from Kindergarten into the Adult Years* (New York: John Wiley & Sons, 1973).

2. Advanced Placement (AP) tests exist for these subjects:

Art	German
Art History	Government and politics (American)
Biology	Government and politics (comparative)
Calculus	History (American)
Chemistry	History (European)
Computer science	Latin
Economics (macro- and micro-)	Music theory
English language and composition	Physics
English literature and composition	Psychology
Environmental Science (as of 1998)	Spanish
French	Statistics

If there isn't an AP test for the subject your child is studying, ask the teacher or counselor if a statewide or nationwide test exists for that subject.

3. Tom Luce, *Now or Never: How We Can Save Our Public Schools* (Dallas: Taylor Publishing, 1995), 42.

4. For example, teachers in New Orleans told reporters they were under pressure to pass unprepared high-school seniors, including those "who can't write a sentence or work simple math problems." Rhonda Nobonne, "Teachers Pushed to Pass, They Say; Administration Defends Tests," *New Orleans Times-Picayune*, May 17, 1996, A1.

5. Andrei Toom, "A Russian Teacher in America," *Journal of Mathematical Behavior* 12 (June 1993): 117-39, quoted in Albert Shanker, "'Pseudo-Education,'" New Republic (November 8, 1993): 11.

6. Seventy-three percent of U.S. 8th graders scored below the "proficient" level on the National Assessment of Educational Progress in 2000. The interpretation of "proficiency" comes from Ina Mullis, John Dossey, Eugene Owen, and Gary Phillips, *The State of Mathematics Achievement: Executive Summary* (Washington, D.C.: National Center for Education Statistics, 1990), 7.

See also *Office of Educational Research and Improvement, Parental Satisfaction with Schools and the Need for Standards* (Washington, D.C.: U.S. Department of Education, November 1992).

7. Judith Anderson, *What Do Grades Mean: Differences across Schools* (Washington, D.C.: Office of Educational Research and Improvement, U.S. Department

of Education, January 1994), available on the Internet at www.ed.gov/pubs/OR/ResearchRpts/grades.html.

Low-income parents' lack of information on their children's school performance was also explored in a separate University of Texas study of one hundred at-risk high-school students. This study found that, although 61 percent of the students' parents believed their children were being prepared for college, only 31 percent of the students graduated from high school by age nineteen, only one student actually went to a four-year college, and that student flunked out the first year! The researchers found that many parents believed their children were doing well as long as they passed their courses and the school did not notify the parents that anything was wrong. Harriett D. Romo and Toni Falbo, Latino High School Graduation: Defying the Odds (Austin: University of Texas Press, 1996), 10 and 43.

8. The state or school district may prevent you from seeing test questions or may ask you to sign an agreement not to reveal the test contents. In any case, they should have a set of sample questions that resemble questions on the test.

9. To be more precise, tests are intended to show what your child has learned in the specific areas covered by the test.

10. According to one study, 25 percent of parents of high-school students did not have any idea how their children were doing in school, and 40 percent never attended a school function, such as a teacher conference or back-to-school night. Meanwhile, 50 percent of students said they do not do the homework they are assigned, two-thirds of students said they had cheated on a school test in the past year, and nine out of ten had copied someone else's homework in the past year. Laurence Steinberg, *Beyond the Classroom: Why School Reform Has Failed and What Parents Need to Do* (New York: Simon and Schuster, 1996).

2

What Should Your Child Learn?

The best education for the best is the best education for all.

— *Robert M. Hutchins, president, University of Chicago*

QUESTIONS ADDRESSED IN THIS CHAPTER

- What are the advantages of having clear, high academic standards?
- How can I tell if my child's school has high academic standards?
- How can I get a first-rate education for my child?
- What does a first-rate education accomplish?
- What should my child learn in preschool and kindergarten?
- What should my child learn in first and second grade?
- What should my child learn in third through fifth grade?
- What should my child learn in sixth through eighth grade?
- What should my child learn by the end of high school?
- What research and study skills should my child learn?
- What nonacademic skills should my child learn?

If you've ever asked the question "Is my child learning as much as she should?" then you've raised the question of standards. Academic standards describe what students should learn and the quality of work they are expected to do. If the school's academic standards are high, then your child is expected to learn a lot and produce high-quality work. (See "Two Kinds of Academic Standards.")

When standards are written in clear language, you can compare what your child is expected to learn with what students in the best schools in the region, the nation, or the world are expected to learn. Standards can inform you about the essentials of a first-rate education. High but attainable academic standards can motivate your child and her teachers to excel (see chapter 6).

When academic standards are low, students become
bored and lose interest in school. The most
talented students are likely to be turned off the most.

TWO KINDS OF ACADEMIC STANDARDS

Content standards describe what your child should learn. Examples: "Your child should learn the multiplication table." "Your child should be able to write an essay discussing the causes of World War I."

Performance standards describe how well your child should learn the material and the quality of work she should produce. "Your child should be able to do at least fifteen multiplication problems, such as 9×6, in one minute, with 100 percent accuracy." A performance standard might give examples of excellent discussions of the causes of World War I, describe the criteria by which the work is judged, and explain why the excellent papers met the standard.

Many individuals and groups write content and performance standards; teachers, schools, school districts, and states adopt them and sometimes attach consequences to them: "The students must meet this standard in order to earn an A." "Students must meet these standards in order to earn a high-school diploma." Because good performance standards are harder to write than content standards, fewer schools and school districts have them.

The word *curriculum* usually means content standards—what the students are expected to know and be able to do. When you ask for a copy of your school's curriculum, the teacher should give you a list of content standards for each subject and grade level. Other times, teachers use the word *curriculum* to mean "instructional program"—the methods they use to teach students in the classroom.

PURPOSES OF EDUCATION

Your child's education should accomplish at least these purposes:

- to enrich her life with the best of human knowledge and culture
- to prepare her to become a responsible, well-informed citizen
- to prepare her for success in her chosen occupation
- to encourage her to become a lifelong learner

WHAT ARE THE ADVANTAGES OF HAVING CLEAR, HIGH ACADEMIC STANDARDS?

To inform parents, students, and the public what a first-rate education looks like. Everyone should be aware that the requirements for a well-educated person in the twenty-first century will be different from and higher than those of the past.

To prevent large numbers of students from receiving an inadequate education. Evidence that millions of Americans are not well educated comes from the National Assessment of Educational Progress and numerous surveys of the knowledge of students and adults.[1] There is no evidence of a past "golden age" in which most of our population was well educated. In earlier times, most students dropped out before the end of high school and found jobs requiring few skills.

To motivate students and educators by giving them ambitious goals. If students and teachers aim higher, they are likely to accomplish more.

Good Content Standards
Set priorities for what is most important to learn. Listing everything that is desirable to know could fill an entire library. At the same time, content standards should not dictate methods to teachers and

should allow room for students to pursue their own interests and explore topics in depth while meeting the knowledge and skill requirements of an educated person.

Emphasize the "big ideas" that are essential to understanding an academic discipline, such as history, geography, civics, or chemistry. For example, one set of standards identifies fifty-six ideas essential to understanding modern biology. Standards should also emphasize the most important skills, such as reading, writing, thinking, research, and presentation skills and setting up and solving mathematical problems.[2] Students must also learn a core of factual information—for example, it's hard to evaluate the impact of the Great Depression if you know nothing about what happened.

Avoid unnecessary "either/or" choices in education: *either* memorizing the multiplication table or solving complex mathematical problems; *either* teaching a core curriculum *or* encouraging students to pursue their own interests. In feeding our children, we do not say, "*Either* my child gets protein or she gets vitamins." Students need a balanced and varied educational diet.

Are easy for parents, students, and teachers to understand— limited only by their knowledge of the subject matter. Even if you don't understand one of the standards, you can still evaluate your child's learning by asking her to explain it. For example, if a trigonometry standard asks students to "derive the law of sines and the law of cosines and apply these laws in solving problems," you can ask your child if she has studied the law of cosines and can explain it to you.

Provide clear information on what students should learn in each grade level. You should be told what your child is expected to learn by the end of this year.

Are coordinated across grade levels, so that what is taught in third grade prepares students for what they will learn in fourth grade.

Good Performance Standards
Make it easy for parents and teachers to tell when students have met the standard. Avoid vague standards, such as "The student will construct personal meaning from her own reading experiences."

Allow for multiple performance levels. We should distinguish between satisfactory, good, and excellent performance.

HOW CAN I TELL IF MY CHILD'S SCHOOL HAS HIGH ACADEMIC STANDARDS?

First you must learn what the school's content and performance standards are:

Request a copy of the school's curriculum to learn about the content standards for each grade level. The school office should have a copy, as should every teacher. Some schools also keep a copy in the school library. If these standards aren't clear, ask for clarification.

Some schools don't have a written curriculum, and others don't provide every teacher with a copy of the curriculum. Lack of a curriculum may mean that the school doesn't have clear standards for what students are expected to learn. In this case, you may want to get involved in the district planning process to establish these standards (see chapter 11).

Talk to the teachers about what their students are expected to learn.

Ask for examples of excellent, good, and satisfactory work in the subjects and grade levels you're interested in to learn about performance standards. Find out whether these standards are set by individual teachers or by the teachers in a subject or grade level working together. You may have already done this if you asked your child's teacher to show examples of A and B work (see chapter 1).

If the school uses portfolio assessment (discussed in chapter 3), then samples of excellent, good, and satisfactory work—created by students or teachers—should be available as public documents.

Once you have learned about the school's standards, evaluate them:

Use your own judgment about whether the school appears to require high-quality work from the students.

Compare the school's standards with those in the best schools you can find, locally, regionally, and nationally.

Compare the school's standards with nationally or internationally recognized standards. The Core Knowledge Foundation, Virginia Department of Education, and New Standards Project have developed some of these standards. See the appendix for more information.

Find out how students who meet the high school's standards do on Advanced Placement tests in the same subject. These tests examine your child's ability to do college-level work in specific subject areas. Do the high school's A students do well on these tests?

Find out how students who meet the school's standards do later in school, college, or the workplace. Do the elementary or middle school's A students do well in middle or high school? Do the high school's A students do well in college? Do employers find the A students well prepared?

Show work that meets the school's standards to teachers at the next higher level of education. For example, show samples of work that meets the elementary school's standards to teachers in excellent middle schools.

Show work that meets the high school's standards to employers who pay high wages. (See "How to Talk to Employers about Your School's Standards.")

HOW TO TALK TO EMPLOYERS ABOUT YOUR SCHOOL'S STANDARDS

Here are some ways to get feedback from business and community leaders about your child's work and about the school's samples of excellent work:

Job fairs: You can speak with local and national business representatives at job fairs and show them your child's best writing samples and work projects. Ask them whether her work would be considered high quality at their businesses. Do the same with work representing the school standards.

Meetings with scholarship sponsors: Contact local businesses that sponsor scholarships and offer well-paying jobs and ask to speak with the coordinator of the scholarship program. Such local organizations as the Rotary Club and any school adopters will probably be happy to have members review work samples.

PTA-sponsored events: Ask your PTO or PTA to sponsor a special event with local businesses who are willing to critique work samples and speak with parents.

Discuss the matter with your child
before showing her work to others.

HOW CAN I GET A FIRST-RATE EDUCATION FOR MY CHILD?

Learn about what students with a first-rate education should know and be able to do. See questions 4 through 11 and the sources in the appendix.

Identify the courses and schools where students are expected to learn the most. Teachers or the school counselor should be able to tell you what those schools and courses are. If your school doesn't offer the courses, consider moving your child to a school that does (see chapter 4).

Enroll your child in the most advanced courses. Find out what she needs to do to prepare for these courses—and make sure she does it.

Beware of low expectations. If your child is encouraged
to take easy, unchallenging courses, that
could be a sign that she's not expected to learn much.
Make sure your own expectations are high as well.

Avoid courses that have low standards. Some schools enroll large numbers of students in courses where the students don't learn much. (See "What Are Warning Signs of Courses with Low Standards?")

WHAT ARE WARNING SIGNS OF COURSES WITH LOW STANDARDS?

It may not always be obvious that a course has low standards. Sometimes courses are labeled "honors" or "college preparatory" but the students are not covering advanced material. Warning signs include:

- Students do not find the work challenging.
- The level of work seems below that of courses in the best schools.
- Students are mostly reviewing material they had in previous years.
- Students are bored or disinterested.
- Students have little or no homework.
- Students are rarely asked to write, do research, or solve problems.

It's important to recognize these warning signs early since it's often difficult for your child to change classes in the middle of the year.

WHAT DOES A FIRST-RATE EDUCATION ACCOMPLISH?

A first-rate education prepares your child to do college-level work by the end of high school and optimally by tenth grade. A first-rate education introduces her to the best of human knowledge and culture and prepares her for successful work, citizenship, and lifelong learning.

A good indication of your child's ability to do college-level work is her ability to do well in Advanced Placement courses and tests.

The rest of this chapter describes a challenging, academically advanced curriculum that establishes ambitious goals for all students. Academically delayed students will need help catching up in order to master this curriculum. (See chapters 5 and 6.)

What should your child learn by the end of high school if you want her to have an excellent education, not just a minimum education?

Your child should master the basics of reading, writing, and arithmetic in elementary school. She should leave elementary school with the ability to read a newspaper and share knowledge about the persons and places she reads about; to write a clear letter or essay describing an event or stating a point of view; to use correct grammar, spelling, punctuation, and appropriate choice of words; and to solve mathematical problems involving whole numbers, fractions, decimals, percentages, ratios, exponents, roots, probabilities, and graphs.[3]

In **mathematics** she should master first-year algebra by eighth grade and at least a year of calculus by twelfth grade. She should be familiar with probability and statistics and with mathematical reasoning and proofs. She should be able to solve complex problems that require several steps and to present and explain her solutions.

In **science** she should be able to use scientific methods of investigation; be familiar with important scientific theories and ideas; be aware of the nature and importance of current scientific research; and use mathematics to make predictions and describe scientific ideas. She should also be able to describe how modern technology uses scientific knowledge.

In **English** she should read great literature—which has moved and inspired people over many generations—and be able to discuss why people have found this literature worthwhile. She should be able to present her ideas clearly in written essays and oral presentations and be encouraged to express herself through poetry and creative writing. She should be able to read and discuss college-level material.

She should learn at least one **foreign language** well: be able to speak and understand the language well, write in that language using proper grammar and word usage, and read and appreciate literature in that language.

Talk to local school officials about the availability
and funding of foreign language instruction.

She should understand **history** as a story of human success and failure. She should be able to describe what happened in various parts of the world during different historical eras and discuss the importance of those events. She should know economic history and the history of science and technology. She should be able to describe how historians do research, conduct research on her own, and evaluate that research.

In **geography** she should know the location of countries, cities, geographic features (such as mountains, rivers, and lakes), climatic zones, natural resources, and important industries. She should be able to create maps; interpret information from maps, satellite-produced images, and geographic information systems; and explain why cities, industries, and climatic zones are where they are. She should be able to discuss how geographic features or barriers have affected the course of history.

Her learning about **civics and government** should give her the ability to explain theories of the role of government, responsibilities of citizens, civil society, political rights, laws and constitutions, campaigns and elections, functions of the branches of government, the separation of powers, the U.S. constitution, and how government policies are developed.

In **economics** she should learn about supply and demand, productivity and efficiency, opportunity cost, consumption, saving, investment, inflation, unemployment, international trade, comparisons of market prices with social costs and benefits, and the successes and failures of markets and government.

Her learning about **society and culture** should give her a strong understanding of not only her own but also other people's cultures and a good understanding of what human beings have in common.

She should become knowledgeable about the **fine arts** of music, theater, dance, and the visual arts. She should be familiar with materials, tools, and techniques of each type of art and learn about art, music, drama, and dance of different styles from different historical periods. She should develop skills in one or more of the arts and understand their importance in communicating human imagination and emotion.

The following sections provide examples of what
your child should learn—not a complete list.
Her school should give you a more detailed list
of what she is expected to learn in each grade.

WHAT SHOULD MY CHILD LEARN
IN PRESCHOOL AND KINDERGARTEN?

A good preschool or kindergarten program addresses the needs of all children, is respectful of differences among them, and offers a curriculum that encourages young children's natural curiosity, creativity, and love of learning. In the process, your child should develop important skills in the following areas: oral language, prereading skills, early writing and math skills, thinking skills, drama and art, movement and muscular coordination, health and personal hygiene, social skills, and good habits and character.[4] You can also help teach these skills at home.

Oral Language

Your child should learn how to talk in full sentences and explain what she is thinking, to recount recent events or the events in a story in order, to make up and tell her own stories, to describe how to do something, and to understand and carry out multistep directions (go upstairs, get the broom and dustpan out of the closet, and clean up the spilled corn flakes). You can help your child develop these skills by talking to her and *listening to her.*

Prereading Skills

These are important skills for your child to learn in order to become ready to read by kindergarten or first grade. Most schools teach these skills in kindergarten; many parents and preschools introduce them before kindergarten.

Letter names and sounds. By the end of kindergarten—ideally in preschool—she should learn the names of the letters and the sounds they make. She should be able to recognize and name all of the uppercase and lowercase letters. Knowing the sounds is also important in learning to read. For example, knowing the sounds of the letters *m*, *a*, and *n* is important for reading the word man, whereas knowing the letter names is less helpful—"em-ay-enn" does not say *man*.

> The letters of the alphabet should be your child's
> familiar friends by the time she enters first grade,
> and ideally when she enters kindergarten.

Sound awareness. She should learn how to hear three separate sounds in the word *cat*. This is separate from knowing letter sounds: she can hear the /k/ sound in cat without knowing that the letter *c* makes that sound. She should also be able to hear separate syllables in multisyllable words.[5]

Reading nursery rhymes and Dr. Seuss books to your child teaches sound awareness. (Children become more aware of sounds when they rhyme words.) You can also play word games, such as "Think of as many words as you can that rhyme with *cat*" or "Think of as many words as you can that go with cat, cow, cup, card, and cape." She should begin learning sound awareness in preschool in order for this skill to be well developed by the end of kindergarten.

Familiarity with books and other printed matter. She should learn that the story in a book comes from the words, not just the pictures; that words are separated by spaces; and that print reads from left to right. (Young children usually don't know left from right, but they can point to the way that the print goes.) She may also "pretend read" stories that she knows by heart.

> Begin reading to your child when she is
> an infant. Read to her every day.

Beginning Reading Skills

Although many schools don't teach beginning reading skills until first grade, your child can benefit from being introduced to these skills in kindergarten.[6] (See "Important Beginning Reading Skills" in the discussion of first grade below.)

Some educators prefer to deemphasize early reading. They fear that the following will happen: a) children will be pressured to learn to read before they are able; b) this will make them frustrated and discouraged; and c) as a result, they will lose interest in reading.

You can avoid this problem by paying close attention to your child's motivation. Is she enthusiastic about reading? Encourage her enthusiasm by reading to her and showing interest in reading yourself. Encourage her interest in reading but do not force the issue or show disappointment if she's not ready (See "Is Your Child Ready to Read?").

IS YOUR CHILD READY TO READ?

Your child will probably not be ready to read until she has begun to learn letter sounds and can hear separate sounds in words. Good ways to tell if she is ready include the following:

- As you read to her, show her how to use the letter sounds to figure out what one or two of the words say. If she's interested in trying to figure out some words herself and has some success with the easiest words, she's probably ready.
- Get a set of beginning reading lessons that teach children how to blend letter sounds together to make words. Try a lesson and see if it's easy to hold your child's interest (see the appendix).

If your child isn't ready, she will usually show this by a clear lack of interest in trying to read. Pay attention to these signals. However, you should also pay attention to those "teachable moments" when she is curious about reading and other subjects.

Some educators also oppose teaching reading and other "academic" skills in kindergarten on the belief that the *methods* used to teach these skills will not be appropriate for young children.[7] Yet good teachers are able to find good ways to teach these skills.

Early Writing Skills

Your child should be encouraged to "pretend write" letters or notes and try to write letters and spell words. If the misspellings she makes are phonetic ("wuz" or "wz" for "was," for example), then that's a good sign that she knows the letter sounds. It's also good for her to develop an interest in how words are actually spelled.

Young children may reverse letters, substituting *b* for *d*, for example, and often have trouble holding a pencil and forming the letters. Most of these problems should disappear by the end of second grade as your child matures.

Early Math Skills

Your preschool child should be given opportunities to count objects and should be shown how to count them without skipping or double counting. Over time, she will develop "number sense"—the awareness that five objects are five objects, no matter how you arrange them, and that any five objects can be matched one-to-one with five other objects. She will be able to tell that row B has fewer dots than row A, but that row C has the same number of dots as row A.

Row A • • • • •

Row B • • • • •

Row C • • • • •

Your child can learn to do such problems as 5 + 3 and 6 – 4 using small objects, such as pennies or pieces of breakfast cereal. She can learn to count up to one hundred objects, grouping them by sets of ten, and noticing the patterns of repetition when she counts.[8] By the end of kindergarten, she should read numbers and begin to look for number patterns on a hundred-square:

1	2	3	4	5	6	7	8	9	10
11	12	13	14	15	16	17	18	19	20
21	22	23	24	25	26	27	28	29	30
31	32	33	34	35	36	37	38	39	40
41	42	43	44	45	46	47	48	49	50
51	52	53	54	55	56	57	58	59	60
61	62	63	64	65	66	67	68	69	70
71	72	73	74	75	76	77	78	79	80
81	82	83	84	85	86	87	88	89	90
91	92	93	94	95	96	97	98	99	100

Once she has mastered the hundred-square, she can begin learning about place value. For example, she can learn how to represent the number 53 with five tens and three ones.

Science

Exposure to scientific ideas and experiences should begin in preschool as your child observes interesting events in nature; hears stories about dinosaurs, volcanoes, and hurricanes; collects plants, bugs, and rocks; plays with tuning forks, colored filters, lenses, and magnets; and repeatedly asks "why?" You can pose "why" questions to her to encourage the process. Some of these should be questions you don't know the answers to, so that she understands that adults have the same sense of wonder that she does.

Computer Skills

Your child should become familiar with computers and begin playing educational computer games. Even in preschool she can learn how to start up and quit programs and manipulate objects on the screen. She should use accurate terminology for the parts of the computer.

Thinking Skills

Your child should begin learning how to distinguish fantasy from reality in books and television. If she watches television, it's important to discuss how many of the dramatic events shown are make-believe but look real. She should become aware of cause and effect in the world.

History and Geography

Your child should learn about local history and geography: where important local landmarks are found and interesting local events that happened in the past. She should also begin learning about faraway times and places. She should learn the names of the seven continents and something important and interesting about each one. She should hear stories about famous people and places in history and about how different groups of people came to the United States. The purpose is not to create a full understanding of where and when everything occurred—this will come later—but to excite her curiosity and desire to learn about places and events.

Drama and Art

Art for your preschool child can include drawing, coloring, painting, modeling with clay, and making objects with paper or Popsicle sticks. She should participate in activities in which she pretends to be other people or characters in a story. She should listen to different kinds of music, be familiar with different kinds of musical instruments, and have opportunities to begin playing an instrument. She should also have opportunities to participate in different kinds of dance.

Movement and Muscular Coordination

Your child should participate in activities that teach her to control her movements, to balance, and to handle a ball; to manipulate small objects with her hands; and to be able to swim.

Health and Safety

Your child should know her own address and telephone number, the name of the doctor or health care clinic that takes care of her, and how to ask for help in an emergency. She should know what to do if she is lost; know about common safety hazards inside and outside of the home; and know how to prevent injuries and avoid unsafe situations. She should be familiar with and practice personal hygiene:

cleanliness, washing hands, brushing teeth, and other personal care. She should know names and functions of parts of the body and be aware of personal privacy. She should give examples of foods that are healthy to eat and know that shots protect her from certain kinds of illness.

Social Awareness and Social Skills

Your child should develop awareness of her own and other people's feelings. She should be able to describe emotions, such as sadness, anger, and frustration, and develop ways of coping with these emotions. She should learn how to negotiate with other children and take turns, to show good manners, and to wait her turn when speaking. You can help her develop these skills by modeling them yourself, talking about how you deal with situations, and encouraging her when she shows concern for other people or resolves conflict well.

Good Habits and Character

Your child should be encouraged to think about the consequences of what she and other people do; bad acts are bad because they have bad consequences. She should begin learning the importance of being honest and following the Golden Rule. (Treat others the way you would like to be treated—not necessarily the way you actually are treated.) She should learn the beginnings of responsibility: how to finish tasks and clean up, to take care of animals and possessions, and to postpone gratification.

Your child learns from what you do, not just from what you say.

WHAT SHOULD MY CHILD LEARN IN FIRST AND SECOND GRADE?

Reading

By the beginning of first grade, your child should have the prereading skills discussed in the previous section. If not, read and play word games with her. Having these skills greatly improves her chances of becoming a good reader.

Early reading skills. By the middle of first grade, she should be able to read words and books she has never seen before. By the middle of second grade, she should be able to read "chapter books"—books with several chapters and lots of words. A desirable goal is for your first-grader to read about one hundred little books and your second-grader to read at least twenty-five longer books written at her grade level or above. Read to her and encourage her to read every day.

To become a good reader, she will need to learn how to sound out unfamiliar words, read word families and sight words, and notice unusual spelling patterns in English. Some children seem to catch on to reading without any instruction in these skills; most children benefit from having the skills explicitly taught.[9] (See "Important Beginning Reading Skills.")

IMPORTANT BEGINNING READING SKILLS

Learning to read is like learning to ride a bicycle without training wheels—the hardest part is getting started. Once she starts reading, the best way for your child to read better is to read a lot. Instruction in several basic reading skills can help her get started:

Sounding out words. While pointing to the letters in M-A-N, show her how to blend their sounds together: "mmmm-maaaaannnnn." Then show her how to "say it fast" as man.

Word families. If she knows letter sounds and can read the word man, she can figure out how to read fan, tan, and ran.

Sight words. Many of the most common words in English, such as "to" and "of," aren't spelled the way they sound and must be learned as whole words.

Interesting spellings and sounds. Your child should be able to identify silent letters in such words as *light* and *comb*; be aware of how an *e* added to the end of *cap* changes the sound of the *a*; notice that *from* and *come* aren't spelled alike, even though they rhyme, but that *come* and *home* are spelled alike, even though they *don't* rhyme.

Paying attention to the meaning. If she pays attention to the meaning while she reads, she should be able to figure out some words from the context: " He turned out the li—" becomes "He turned out the light" even if she has trouble sounding out the rest of the word *light*. She should catch most of her own mistakes when she reads.

Encourage your child to sound out unknown words, not just guess them. She needs to learn to read what's actually on the page. Using the context is important when sounding out words yields ambiguous results, as in the sentence: "The prospector offered to *lead* us to the *lead* deposits." If your child misreads a word and the sentence doesn't make sense as a result, remind your child to "make it make sense."

See chapter 5 for ways to improve your child's reading skills.

If your child falls behind, she could be a "late bloomer" who will catch up without extra help. However, the safe choice is to get her tutored, which will help her whether or not she is a late bloomer (see chapter 5). Do not assume that she has a learning disability just because she is a late reader. Also, do not assume she is a late bloomer if she reads late—she may have missed important prereading skills.

Literature. She should be introduced to good literature: stories, fables, poetry, legends, and myths that have excited, inspired, and entertained people through the ages. Be introduced to the elements of a story (main character, setting, problem, and solution); be able to predict what will probably happen next; and be able to describe feelings, thoughts, and motivations of characters. Distinguish fantasy from reality and identify themes and main ideas.

Writing

Composition. By the end of first grade, your child should be able to write complete sentences that begin with a capital letter and end with correct punctuation. Be able to generate ideas and get them down on the page. Daily writing assignments, such as keeping a journal, often help with this process.

By the end of second grade, write stories, letters, and short summaries of what she saw or read; these should consist of several paragraphs with a beginning, middle, and end. Edit her own writing to correct spelling, capitalization, grammar, and punctuation errors.

Spelling. Begin learning how to spell in first grade. By the end of second grade, be able to spell phonetically regular words and frequently used irregular words.

Handwriting. Handwriting instruction in first grade should emphasize legibility. She should be taught how to form the letters correctly and space letters and words appropriately. Learn to write in cursive by the end of second grade.

Oral Language

Your child should learn to tell stories, express her ideas and feelings clearly, listen to others respectfully, and describe what she has seen or learned. For example, she might show another child how to do a math problem, tell the class about a book she has read, describe an insect she found, and be able to ask appropriate questions of a visiting author, firefighter, or scientist.

Mathematics

Your child should learn about place value, addition, subtraction, multiplication, division, measurement and geometry, mental arithmetic, probability and statistics, fractions, and patterns and relationships.

Whole number operations and place value. By the end of second grade, she should be able to say how many tens, hundreds, or thousands are in a number and count up or down by thousands, hundreds, tens, or ones (3,200, 3,300, 3,400 ...). Know when to add, subtract, multiply, and divide and understand relationships among these operations; memorize addition and subtraction facts up to 9 + 9 and 18 − 9; add and subtract with regrouping (carrying and borrowing); count by twos, threes, fours, fives, and tens; and know the multiplication tables for 0, 1, 2, 5, and 10.

Problem solving. Solve word problems that require one or two steps and show more than one way to solve a problem. Represent a problem in more than one way; for example, 24 + 35 can be shown as 4 + 5 + 20 + 30 or 24 + 5 + 30, as a story problem, with pictures of twenty-four and thirty-five objects, or with actual objects. Explain how she got the answer.

Fractions. Understand that one-fourth is the result obtained when a circle, square, or rectangle is divided into four equal parts. Recognize relationships between fractions; for example, half of one-fourth is one-eighth.

Estimation and mental arithmetic. Spot when addition and subtraction problems produce answers that are not reasonable, for example, 38 + 56 = 814; come up with sensible estimates of the number of feet across the room or the number of raisins in a box; and add and subtract numbers, such as 38 + 64 and 42 - 18, in her head.

Measurement and geometry. Understand the difference between two- and three-dimensional shapes and be able to combine or split up shapes to make other shapes. Measure and estimate length, area, and volume and explain the advantage of using standard units of measure. (For example, how much is "five cups" if everyone uses a different size cup?) Tell time to the minute on a conventional clock.

Probability and statistics. Make and interpret a simple bar or line graph. Predict which of two events is more likely to occur and explain why; for example, if a box of ten balls and another box of one hundred balls each has one red ball, from which box are you more likely to draw a red ball?

Patterns and relationships. Identify the next number in a sequence, such as 1, 3, 6, 10, ?; identify the unknown number in the sentence 16 - □ = 7; identify pairs of numbers that satisfy the rule □ + _ = 10.

Science

Your child should do hands-on activities that prepare her to learn scientific ideas. She should be encouraged to read children's science books and begin learning about scientific method—the ways scientists gather information and test their ideas—and about scientific content—what we have learned about the world. By the end of second grade, she should be able to do the following:

Scientific method. Conduct scientific experiments. A sample experiment might compare two groups of plants that are the same, except that one group gets more sunlight.

Physical science. Be able to name common examples of solids, liquids, and gases and explain how water changes from one state to another; explain that vibrating objects make sound; describe ways that sound, heat, light, and electricity can travel; show how magnets can push or pull on each other; put together a simple electric circuit using a battery, wires, and a lightbulb.

Life science. Explain the importance of plants to life on earth. Draw a diagram of a food chain. Draw a picture of a habitat, such as a forest or marsh; describe some of the animals and plants that live there; and discuss some of the ways that they depend on each other. Discuss life in the oceans. Describe different families of animals and plants, such as mammals, birds, reptiles, and insects. Discuss the life cycle of insects and flowering plants. Describe ways in which she resembles her parents and siblings. Know about the functions of skin, bones, muscles, heart, lungs, digestive organs, blood, nerves, and the brain. Know something about the long history of life on earth and explain how fossils are used to infer what prehistoric plants and animals were like.

Earth science and astronomy. Describe some of the ways that rocks are formed. Talk about what causes earthquakes and volcanoes. Describe the water cycle—evaporation, condensation, and precipitation. Know that the moon goes around the earth and the earth goes around the sun. Explain the causes of tides, seasons, and phases of the moon. Know about planets and other objects in the solar system and be able to say where outside the earth humans have actually gone.

Teachers will not be able to teach about each of these science topics in a single year, but all this and more should be touched on sometime between kindergarten and the end of second grade.

Foreign Language

Your child should be taught how to express her needs and describe everyday objects and events in a foreign language. Children who come from non-English speaking homes should be completely fluent in English by third grade—or after three years in American schools if they are recent immigrants.

Computer Skills

By second grade, your child should be familiar with computer terminology, such as cursor, open, close, windows, and the menu bar. She should be able to choose a program, use it, and quit; copy and paste information from one application to another; and save and retrieve files that she creates. During word processing she should be able to edit text and change its font, style, and size. She should be introduced to touch typing on a computer keyboard and begin learning how to use computers to search for information.

Thinking Skills

Your child should know how to sort and classify objects: "Pick out the objects that are round and are either red or blue." She should be encouraged to think of different conclusions that could follow from what she observes; for example, "Joe's car isn't in the garage, so maybe Joe isn't home, or he's home but his car is in the shop or is being used by someone else."

History

Your child should read and hear stories about famous historical events; become acquainted with leaders in many fields; and learn the qualities that great people possess and the changes they caused to happen. She should know about the Lincoln Memorial, the Washington Monument, the Statue of Liberty, and the Seven Wonders of the ancient world. She should begin learning about ancient civilizations in Egypt, Greece, and Rome. Time lines should be introduced so that even the very young child can begin to see the sequence of events and changes that have occurred over time.

Geography

Your child should begin learning the locations of cities, states, and countries and of important geographic features: continents, oceans, rivers, lakes, and deserts. For example, your second-grader should be able to locate the seven continents and four oceans on a world map and locate several countries in South America, Europe, Africa, and Asia. She should learn about local geography; be able to find her own street, neighborhood, and important local geographic features on a map; and be able to describe the city or community, state, and nation where she lives.

Civics and Government

Your child should be able to explain the importance of rules that are applied fairly to everyone and discuss how rules are made and why governments are necessary. She should be familiar with what government does in her community and how citizens pay for government services.

Economics

Your child should understand that goods, services, natural resources, and time exist in limited supply; that a choice to do or buy one thing involves not doing or buying other things; and that there are different ways to divide up society's income and wealth. She should be able to explain why many people specialize in doing one thing and why sellers advertise their products and must please their customers.

Society and Culture

Your child should hear stories about people in different parts of the world. She should be introduced to literature, music, art, and customs of different societies. She should be able to give examples of things that people in different societies do differently but also understand that people everywhere have many of the same desires and emotions she does.

Fine Arts

Your child should learn to appreciate different kinds of music and art. She should have opportunities to paint, draw, model, and build with different art materials; begin learning to read music and play a musical instrument; learn different styles of dance; and participate in class and school plays.

Health and Fitness

Your child should have the information she needs to get help in an emergency and to recognize dangerous situations. She should be introduced to traffic, fire, water, and recreation safety. She should know about habits that keep herself healthy and be able to describe types of food that are important for a good diet. She should participate in individual and team sports, swimming, and gymnastics.

WHAT SHOULD MY CHILD LEARN
IN THIRD THROUGH FIFTH GRADE?

Reading

By the middle of third grade, your child should be able to read multisyllable words, such as intermediate, exhilarated, unbelievable, or navigator. Reading third-grade books should require little effort. By fifth grade, she should be reading newspapers, magazines, short stories, poems, novels, and children's versions of literary classics. A desirable goal is for your third-, fourth-, or fifth-grader to read at least twenty-five books a year written for children in her grade level or above. To acquire important background information, she should read books about history and science as well as storybooks.[10]

She should be able to use prefixes, suffixes, and root words to figure out the meaning of unfamiliar words; use a dictionary, encyclopedia, glossary, and thesaurus; and do research in libraries and on the Internet.[11] Discuss the main idea of a reading passage and, when collecting information about a specific topic, identify the parts that are important to read.

Writing

By fifth grade, your child should be able to write a two- or three-page paper with a clear beginning, middle, and end; vary the sentence structure; revise her writing for clarity; and edit the final draft for grammar, capitalization, spelling, and punctuation. Know how to say in her own words what someone else wrote.

She should be able to write stories and poetry and produce different kinds of nonfiction writing about the same idea: for example, a personal narrative about trying out for a sports team, a how-to guide on how to try out for the team, and a letter advocating making tryouts more (or less) selective.[12] Explain the reasons for her opinion, taking opposing viewpoints into account.

> Your child will have a better chance of writing well in fifth grade if she writes often in first through fourth grades.

Oral Language

Your child should be able to give an oral presentation that communicates a clear message and that has a beginning, middle, and end. Listen to others' presentations, asking clear questions and making relevant comments. Summarize information and ideas clearly.

Mathematics

Your child should learn about computation, problem-solving, measurement and geometry, probability and statistics, and prealgebra.

Whole number operations and place value. Know the relationship among thousands, millions, billions, and trillions; memorize the multiplication table; add, subtract, multiply, and divide numbers with pencil and paper and check the answer; factor numbers into primes ($12 = 3 \times 2 \times 2$); be familiar with exponents and square roots.

Problem solving. Solve word problems involving addition, subtraction, multiplication, and division; solve problems that require several steps; recognize the information needed to solve a problem; and develop multiple solutions to problems that have more than one right answer. Know several strategies for solving a problem.

Fractions, decimals, and percentages. Add, subtract, multiply, and divide fractions, decimals, and percentages. Reduce fractions to their simplest form ($3/6 = \frac{1}{2}$). Convert fractions to decimals or percentages and vice versa. Understand place value for decimals. Use ratios and proportions.

Estimation and mental arithmetic. Calculate and estimate simple multiplication and division problems in her head. Devise procedures to estimate large numbers, such as the number of grains of sand in a sandbox or the number of paces from San Francisco to New York City.

Measurement and geometry. Calculate perimeter, area, and volume; calculate the radius and circumference of a circle; use English and metric units of measurement and convert between the two; measure and estimate angles.

Probability and statistics. Estimate probabilities by listing and counting all of the possible outcomes or by using simple formulas. Understand that it's easier to make predictions about large numbers of people than about individuals. Discuss sources of error in these predictions. Collect and plot data in various ways. Discuss reasons why a sample might not represent the population from which it is drawn.

Patterns, functions, and prealgebra. Distinguish statements that are true for all numbers ($\Box$ + _ = _ + $\Box$), true for some numbers (_ + _ = 10), true for only one number ($\Box$ + 3½ = 10), and never true ($\Box$ × 0 = 10). Write an algebraic sentence to describe the solution to a problem; for example, if s is the number of socks in p pairs, then $s = 2p$. Graph pairs of numbers that satisfy a simple equation, such as y = 2x + 4.

Science

Your child should read science books, do hands-on science activities, and visit science museums, planetariums, and nature areas. You may see her become fascinated by science.

Scientific method. By the end of fifth grade, she should be able to discuss how to set up a controlled experiment and distinguish between hypotheses, observations, inferences, and predictions. Collect data and discuss which ideas the data support; for example, the hypothesis "Hotter water holds more dissolved sugar" leads to the prediction that more sugar will dissolve in 110°F than in 70° water. Make predictions based on a series of observations; for example, predict how much sugar will dissolve in 100° water based on observations of 40°, 60°, and 80° water.

Physical science. Know about matter; forces and inertia; simple machines; atoms and molecules; protons, neutrons and electrons;

chemical change; types of energy; and energy conservation. Use concepts of physical science to explain everyday events, for example, why the sky is blue and sunsets are red; why ice-cream makers use salt water to freeze ice cream; why sweating cools people off; why mirages occur; and why you can estimate how far away lightning is by timing the delay between the lightning flash and the thunderclap.

Life science. Know about the systems of the human body; the causes of various types of diseases; what cells are and what the cell nucleus does; photosynthesis and cell respiration; genes and DNA; adaptation, natural selection, and evolution; different kinds of pollution and their effects on various kinds of living organisms; and costs and benefits of species preservation.

Earth science and astronomy. Know about warm and cold fronts and high and low pressure; explain why it's colder high up in the atmosphere, even though hot air seems to rise; know about rocks and minerals, surface water and groundwater, ocean currents, and the ocean depths; know about the movement of continents over time; know about the solar system and about distances to planets and stars; and know about nebulae and galaxies.

Foreign Language

By fifth grade, your child should be able to ask for or understand anything in a foreign language that a typical three-year-old could in her native language. Be able to write a clear and grammatically correct paragraph in the language.

This presupposes that your school has a strong emphasis on foreign language instruction in elementary school, as many European nations do.

Computer Skills

By the end of fifth grade, your child should be able to use simple word processing, spreadsheet, graphics, and database programs and type information with reasonable speed (fifteen to twenty words per minute). Incorporate information created in one program into another. Be proficient at searching for information on the Internet.

Thinking Skills

Your child should be able to make inferences from "or," "and," and "if . . . then" statements and statements that use "all," "most," "some," and "none." For example, what information is needed to contradict the statement that "all students eat corn and carrots?" How is this different from the information needed to disprove that "all students eat corn *or* carrots?"

She should learn to recognize techniques of persuasion in advertising and everyday life, make distinctions between fact and opinion, and discuss what kinds of evidence would be needed to support a point of view.

History

Your child should read and hear stories of great historical events and important people in history from a variety of eras. Distinguish myths and fictional accounts—in stories, television, and movies—from events that really happened.

By fifth grade, she should be able to put important historical eras and events in order on a time line; discuss important events in the history of her state and nation; know about great civilizations that existed in different historical eras; and discuss sources of information that tell us "what really happened" and "what things were like" in the past.

Geography

Your fifth-grader should be able to use a variety of maps, including maps that represent statistical data; construct a map using a scale (for example, a map of the school in which 1 inch = 50 feet); use the scale on a road map to estimate distances between cities; find a feature on a globe by knowing its latitude and longitude; identify states, countries, rivers, and mountain ranges on a map; know about different areas of climate and vegetation, such as tundra, temperate plains and forests, tropical rain forests, and deserts; and locate regions where important crops are grown, where oil is found, or where major religions are more commonly practiced.

Civics and Government

Your fifth-grade child should be able to describe some of the responsibilities of national, state, and local governments; describe an issue or situation in which people disagree over what government should be responsible for; discuss the responsibilities of citizens; explain the difference between limited and unlimited government, using examples of each; and discuss how some societies limit the power of government.

Economics

Your fifth-grader should be able to discuss supply and demand; the scarcity and opportunity cost of resources; profit-making as the goal of business firms; the concepts of productivity and efficiency; the role of money and banks; and inflation and unemployment.

Society and Culture

Your child should be able to give examples of cultural differences and similarities; provide examples of values that are shared in nearly all cultures and discuss likely reasons why those values are shared; describe ways in which people sort themselves into groups; and discuss ways in which people's behavior in groups can differ from the way they would act by themselves.

Fine Arts

She should become familiar with great art and music of different styles from different historical periods; improve her ability to read music and play a musical instrument; and participate in the writing and production of class skits or school plays. Draw, paint, sculpt, and build and begin learning how to use art to communicate ideas or feelings. Be introduced to opera and ballet.

Health and Fitness

Your child should learn traffic, fire, water, and recreation safety. Know the systems of the human body. Describe different causes of disease and give examples of illnesses produced by each cause. Know ways to prevent illness and disease. Describe the importance to health of hygiene, diet, exercise, rest, and avoiding harmful drugs and environmental toxins. Participate in individual and team sports and improve her endurance, muscular coordination, balance, strength, flexibility, and speed; do well in such events as the President's Physical Fitness Challenge.

WHAT SHOULD MY CHILD LEARN IN SIXTH THROUGH EIGHTH GRADE?

Your child may need extra help in order to succeed in an academically challenging middle-school program, such as the one described here. Strong academic preparation in elementary school is important (see chapter 5).

Reading

Every year between sixth and eighth grade, your child should read a variety of novels, poetry, and plays, many of which are renowned as great works of literature; read extensively about history, science, and current affairs; and memorize poetry. For each kind of writing, analyze how the author's style and choice of language are designed to affect the reader and discuss thoughtfully what she's read. Ideally, read around twenty-five books in a year, including two or three on the same subject or by the same author in order to make comparisons. Give thoughtful opinions about what she has read and support those opinions with evidence.

Writing

Your child should write multipage papers in sixth and seventh grades. By the end of eighth grade, present ideas clearly and concisely in a well-organized paper: explain the results of a research project, discuss a set of ideas, or advocate a point of view. The paper should be long enough to show an appreciation of the complexity of the issue. She should edit her work for spelling, grammar, punctuation, word usage, logical presentation, and readability. Her writing should be able to capture and hold the reader's attention.

Oral Language

Your child should be able to give a clear oral presentation on a paper or project, using appropriate visual aids. In the classroom, participate in small group discussions and summarize the group's conclusions to the class. Make thoughtful comments in class discussions and ask probing questions.

Mathematics

Your child should learn about numbers and operations, problem solving, estimation, mental arithmetic, measurement and geometry, probability and statistics, and patterns and functions. Master elementary algebra by the end of eighth grade.

> Some middle-school students may struggle with algebra — especially if they weren't taught the right prerequisite skills in elementary school. Yet all middle-school students should learn how to set up problems, be aware of the reasons for using symbols, and know the meaning of each symbol. They should be able to answer these questions: What does x stand for? In what units is it measured?

Numbers and operations. Solve problems using whole numbers, fractions, decimals, percentages, ratios, and proportions consistently and correctly; express numbers in scientific notation; solve problems using bases other than 10; use logarithms to calculate 1.05^{10} or $35^{1/3}$ and explain why the method works; and understand similarities and differences between integers and rational and irrational numbers.

Problem solving, estimation, and mental arithmetic. Identify when information needed to solve a problem is missing. Solve problems by working backward or by recognizing similarities with other familiar types of problems. Devise ways to solve multistep problems. Discuss whether an estimate or an exact solution is more appropriate; in the case of an approximate solution, discuss how the answer should be rounded.

Measurement and geometry. Use formulas to calculate the area or volume of two- and three-dimensional shapes. Estimate the area and volume of irregularly shaped objects by breaking them up into smaller shapes. Visualize what shapes look like when they are rotated or flipped. Discuss what affects the accuracy of a measurement and how accurate the measurement needs to be. Determine the number of significant digits in a measurement. Make and use scale drawings.

Probability and statistics. Estimate probabilities by using probability trees or formulas. Calculate the mean and median of a set of numbers and explain what these numbers mean. Give examples to show why the dispersion of a set of numbers matters, not just its mean (for example, people care about how widely temperatures vary in a city throughout the year). Make and interpret different kinds of graphs.

Patterns, functions, and algebra. Use formulas to solve problems (distance = rate × time). Solve problems using inequalities (identify the xs for which $x + 5 < 13$; for which $|x + 5| < 13$). Solve linear equations ($4x + 4 = 2x + 8$) and quadratic equations ($x^2 - 3x + 3 = 0$) where there is one unknown x. Graph such equations as $y = 2x - 1$. Distinguish real from complex numbers. Solve pairs of equations with two unknowns ($y = 2x + 5$ and $y = 3x - 9$). Identify pairs of equations with no solution, one solution, or an infinite number of solutions.

Science

By eighth grade, your child should be familiar with nearly all of the major ideas and theories of modern science—although a good understanding of some of them, such as relativity and quantum physics, may have to wait until high school. You should continue to encourage her to read science books, visit science museums, and do hands-on science activities.

Scientific method. Your child should be able to identify independent and dependent variables in an experiment. (For example, in a pendulum experiment, the dependent variable might be the number of pendulum swings per minute; possible independent variables might include the length of the string, the size and mass of the weight, the height to which the weight is raised, and the length of time the weight has been swinging.) Use repeated trials to establish how much the results are likely to vary due to random chance.

Physical science. Your seventh- or eight-grader should be able to describe what Newton's law of gravity says and explain Newton's three laws of motion, giving examples of how each applies in technology or everyday life.

Know about elements, compounds, and mixtures; the periodic table; chemical reactions; protons, neutrons, and electrons; nuclear energy; the difference between nuclear fission and fusion; radioactivity; the conservation of matter and energy; pressure, buoyancy, and density; sound and light waves, the electromagnetic spectrum, and the Doppler effect; and the relationship between electricity and magnetism.

Use knowledge of science to explain how the following things work: refrigerators and air conditioners, internal combustion engines, hydraulic lifts, airplanes and helicopters, generators and electric motors, photocopying machines, compact disks, transistors and integrated circuits, radio and television, computers, and radar.

Life science. Your eighth-grader should know about cell structure, cell differentiation, cell division, and differences between animal and plant cells; common ways of classifying living things into kingdoms and phyla; different types of microorganisms; inherited and acquired characteristics; DNA and the genetic code; genetic mutation, natural selection, and evolution; relationships among species in an ecosystem; population growth and cycles; the history of life on earth; and different methods used to date rocks and fossils.

Earth science and astronomy. Know about heat transfer in hurricanes and thunderstorms, global climate and weather patterns, theories of global warming and differences in scientific opinion on this matter, ozone depletion, plate tectonics, earthquakes and volcanoes, properties of minerals, and renewable and nonrenewable resources.

Describe the history and technology of space exploration; how stars are believed to evolve, explaining the hypothesized origins of red giants, white dwarfs, and black holes; and the Big Bang theory of the origin of the universe and the evidence that has been used to support that theory.

Foreign Language

Your child should be able to describe common objects and experiences and produce a persuasive essay or give a talk in a foreign language.

> Your child may need a strong foreign language background in elementary school in order to reach this level of performance by the end of eighth grade.

Computer Skills

Your child should be able to use word processing, spreadsheet, graphics, and database programs; incorporate information created in one program into another; search for information in computer networks and databases; and store, retrieve, and transmit electronic information.

Thinking Skills

Your child should understand the importance of asking the right questions. She should be able to recognize techniques of persuasion in political debates and corporate advertising.

She should be quick to spot bad reasoning or poor evidence: false analogies, selective use of evidence, conclusions that don't follow from the information given, conclusions based on nonrepresentative samples or very small sample sizes, appeals to authority ("leading experts say . . ."), and attributions of group stereotypes to individuals ("he's a nerd"). Evaluate the credibility of different accounts of the same event.

History

Your child should be familiar with important events in U.S. and world history—when they occurred and what their importance was. Read two different accounts of the same event and discuss how and why these accounts are different, and how historians try to figure out "what really happened." Compare and contrast events of long ago with those of today; for example, compare the Crusades with modern religious conflicts. Discuss the importance of specific ideas or technological developments in history.

Geography

Your eighth-grader should be able to draw a map of the world, reproducing from memory all of the continents and oceans and most of the major countries, mountain ranges, deserts, and rivers. Use and interpret any kind of map; explain why on some maps Greenland looks almost as big as South America; locate on a map all of the states of the United States, all major countries, and all of the places that are discussed in the news; and locate regions that are more or less economically developed, that are thickly or thinly populated, or that contain various industries and natural resources.

Civics and Government

She should know about the Bill of Rights; the branches of the U.S. government and their responsibilities; the separation of powers; constitutional government; the division of responsibility among local, state, and federal governments; the importance of political and civil rights and the rule of law; and the difference between civil and criminal courts.

Economics

Your eighth-grader should be able to discuss the importance of economic growth, productivity, and income distribution in determining people's standard of living; describe things that increase labor productivity; identify regions in the world where productivity and standards of living are low or high; give examples of how economic incentives affect the behavior of workers and firms; give examples of other influences on economic behavior, such as customs or the desire for social status.

Society and Culture

Your child should be able to discuss why people affiliate into groups; good and bad ways that groups, societies, and institutions can influence the behavior of individuals; and the role of customs, values, and religion in various societies in the world.

Describe the destructive consequences of intergroup conflict, using examples from countries where this conflict has been intense, and discuss ways to resolve conflicts among individuals and groups.

Fine Arts

She should draw, paint, and sculpt using a variety of materials and be given feedback on how to improve her work. Have opportunities to play a musical instrument and understand the importance of practice in improving her own artistic and musical performance. Participate in drama and dance.

Be familiar with great works of art and music from different times and cultures; be able to discuss the historical period and style of these works; and discuss why the works are considered excellent.

Health and Fitness

Your child should be familiar with the systems of the human body, including the functioning of the human immune system. Know about changes that occur in the body with the onset of puberty. Know about ways to prevent illness and disease and discuss risk factors associated with disease. Discuss examples of risky behaviors and know about drugs and toxins, and the risks of addiction to legal and illegal drugs. Be familiar with elementary first aid.

List important nutrients—such as vitamins, protein, starches, sugars, fats, iron, and calcium—discuss what each of these nutrients is good for and give examples of foods rich in these nutrients. Give reasons why too much fat in the diet can be harmful to health. Participate in individual and team sports and improve her endurance, muscular coordination, balance, strength, flexibility, and speed. Do well in events that require physical fitness.

WHAT ABOUT SEX EDUCATION?

Your school or school district should be very interested in parents' opinions on what kind of program to have. A good sex education program might include the following elements:

- Scientific knowledge about the human reproductive system, conception, contraception, and effective ways of preventing sexually transmitted diseases
- Character education, which teaches honesty, responsibility, and respect, and how to resist peer pressure to engage in risky behaviors
- Adult mentoring and guidance on reasons to postpone sexual activity and childbearing

WHAT SHOULD MY CHILD LEARN BY THE END OF HIGH SCHOOL?

Your child may need extra help in order to succeed in an academically challenging high-school program, such as the one described here. Strong academic preparation in elementary and middle school is important (see chapter 5).

Reading
Your child should read great literature and discuss the writer's point of view, the methods the writer used to get the message across, and reasons why the literature is considered great. Distinguish issues that were specific to the writer's time and place from those that have universal importance.

Read articles from the popular, business, and scientific press and be able to discuss the economic, political, and scientific issues they raise.

Read and use technical manuals, instruction books, application forms, warning labels, and flow charts.

Writing

Your child should be able to write for a specific audience, setting, and purpose; an op-ed piece in the newspaper, for example, requires a different writing style than a term paper written for the teacher. Edit her own writing to make it clear and readable and use correct spelling, grammar, punctuation, and choice of words.

Mathematics

Your child should gain experience setting up and solving mathematical problems of various kinds and develop skills in advanced algebra, geometry, trigonometry, precalculus, and calculus.

Problem solving. Construct mathematical proofs when solving problems. Prove something by reasoning from axioms. Prove X by showing that "not X" couldn't be true. Identify whether a particular solution method will work in all situations or just in some situations. Solve multistep problems taken from real-life settings and present and explain her solutions.

Measurement and geometry. Discuss variables that affect the accuracy of a measurement and ways to decide how accurate the measurement needs to be. Use properties of triangles and parallel and perpendicular lines to solve problems and prove theorems.

Advanced algebra and precalculus. Solve equations with two unknowns. Use rectangular and polar coordinates. Know simple rules of matrix algebra and how they can be used to solve systems of linear equations. Work with sequences, series, and limits. Show how the binomial theorem can be used to approximate the number e. Work with exponential and logarithmic functions, polynomials, and complex numbers. Graph functions and identify upper and lower bounds, asymptotes, zeros, y-intercepts, maxima, and minima.

Trigonometry. Find the sine, cosine, tangent, cotangent, secant, and cosecant of an angle; know when enough information is available to do so. Graph these functions and their inverses, and use these functions to solve practical problems.

Probability and statistics. Explain how a polling company can get an accurate estimate of the opinions of millions of voters by surveying only two thousand people. Show how the likely margin of error would increase if the company only surveyed twenty or two hundred people. Use probability distributions to predict how often specific events will occur. Use correlation and regression to examine the relationship between two variables.

Calculus. Distinguish continuous functions; find the first and second derivatives of a function or of the sum, product, quotient, or inverse of a function; apply the chain rule. Find the indefinite integral of a function; approximate the value of a definite integral; use derivatives and integrals to solve real-world problems.

Science

By high-school graduation, your child should understand the most important theories and ideas in every branch of science, practical applications of these ideas, and current research in each major scientific field. For example, she should be able to say what recombinant DNA research is and does, describe several of its applications, discuss policy issues associated with those applications, and discuss one or two major recent research findings in this field.

Scientific method. Compare the merits of alternative experimental designs. Select appropriate units of measure—for example, acceleration is measured in different units than velocity, and force is measured in different units than energy. Express predictions in mathematical form and distinguish between linear and nonlinear relationships. Show knowledge of significant figures and error ranges.

History of science. Describe the history of major theories in science, such as the atomic hypothesis, the theory of evolution, the germ theory of disease, Einstein's modifications of Newtonian physics, and plate tectonics. Describe the evidence on which these theories were based. Distinguish scientific ideas that have changed relatively slowly from areas of research where our understanding has changed quickly.

Technological applications of science. Describe the scientific basis of important technologies, such as lasers, computers, semiconductors, telecommunication, ultrastrong materials, medical imaging, recombinant DNA, monoclonal antibodies, and others as they are developed.

Physics. Analyze inertia, free fall, acceleration, circular motion, kinetic energy, and momentum. Use vectors to represent forces. Discuss how light exhibits wave properties, such as reflection, refraction, diffraction, interference, standing waves, and polarization. Apply Ohm's law in the design of series and parallel circuits. Apply the concepts of specific heat and the latent heat of condensation. Explain the concepts of relativity and quantum theory. Discuss theories of superconductivity and possible uses of superconducting materials.

Chemistry. Discuss different kinds of chemical bonds and chemical reactions and the details of the periodic table. Balance chemical equations, using Avogadro's principle to predict the masses of reactants and products; test these predictions in laboratory experiments. Discuss the use of catalysts to accelerate reaction rates. Apply the concept of chemical equilibrium. Perform calculations and laboratory experiments involving acids and bases and solution concentrations.

Biology. Discuss the functions of different parts of the cell; DNA, RNA, and various kinds of protein; and the components and functioning of the human endocrine and immune systems. Describe how viruses reproduce. Discuss the importance of the Human Genome Project. Discuss the importance of biodiversity, the costs and benefits of species preservation, and the factors affecting species survival.

Earth science and astronomy. Discuss how modern theories explain the location of earthquakes and volcanoes, deposits of important natural resources, and layers of fossil-bearing rocks. Discuss theories and evidence of the age and early history of the universe and the early history of the earth. Describe how stars and galaxies are believed to evolve; evidence for whether the universe is open or closed; and recent discoveries about the solar system.

Foreign Language

Your child should reach a high fluency level in a foreign language, understanding literature and everyday expressions in that language. Be versed in the history, culture, and traditions of societies in which the language is spoken.

Computer Skills

Your child should be proficient in using word processing, spreadsheet, graphics, and database programs; incorporating information created in one program into another; searching for information in computer networks and databases; and using procedures to store, retrieve, and transmit electronic information.

Thinking Skills

Your child should be quick to detect the selective use of evidence to prove a point; conclusions that do not follow from the evidence given; and evidence that supports more than one possible conclusion. Identify techniques used to slant information or lead the reader to a conclusion without supporting that conclusion with logic or evidence. Identify critical assumptions underlying an argument or line of reasoning. Be aware of the human tendency to pay more attention to evidence that supports one's point of view and to apply a higher level of skepticism to evidence that opposes one's point of view.

Distinguish statements that follow logically from those that do not; distinguish conditions that are necessary from those that are both necessary and sufficient; disprove conclusions by the use of counterexamples.

Solve problems by the use of analogies. Solve problems by working backward from possible solutions as well as by working forward or by brainstorming and eliminating possible solutions. Use a balance sheet or decision tree to evaluate the likely costs and benefits of alternative decisions.

History

Your child should be able to discuss why the study of history is important and explain with examples the meaning of the statement "Those who fail to learn from history are condemned to repeat it."

Learn about the history of ideas, the history of technology, economic history, and culture and institutions of societies in the past. Give examples of how changes in technology, ideas, and institutions have affected society. For example, what were the effects of the introduction of irrigation or steam engines? How did monotheistic religion or the ideas of democracy and human rights affect society?

Historical thinking skills. Create and interpret time lines that show the succession of historical events; read documents from a variety of historical sources and evaluate their credibility; distinguish between historical fact and interpretation; analyze cause-and-effect relationships; evaluate arguments of historical inevitability; evaluate major debates among historians about alternative interpretations of the past; and compare events, ideas, and institutions across different eras—for example, compare Athenian democracy with that in a New England town meeting or with U.S. representative democracy. Debate the merits of historical analogies—for example, did the expansionism of Iraq under Saddam Hussein resemble the expansion of Nazi Germany under Hitler?

U.S. history. Discuss the early settlement of the Americas by Europeans and the societies that existed in the Americas before the Europeans arrived; explain why the Americas attracted Europeans and why those Europeans imported slaves from Africa; compare the economies and institutions of the British, French, Spanish, and Portuguese colonies; and describe the competition among European nations for control of North America.

Discuss the history and ideas of the American Revolution and understand the contents of the Declaration of Independence, the U.S. Constitution, and the Federalist Papers. Discuss U.S. territorial expansion, economic growth, and technological progress in the nineteenth century; the Abolitionist movement; the Civil War; and postwar reconstruction. Describe how the U.S. was affected by the rise of corporations, heavy industry, and mechanized farming; by immigration; and by the rise of the labor movement.

Describe changes in U.S. society, politics, and economic conditions in the twentieth century. Discuss events and ideas in the Progressive Era, the period during and immediately after World War I, the 1920s, the Great Depression, and World War II. Describe the importance of the New Deal, the Great Society, and the civil rights movement. Discuss the changing role of the United States in the world; U.S. foreign policy after World War II; the Korean and Vietnam Wars; domestic politics in the postwar period; and current issues facing our society.

World history. Discuss early human communities and the spread of agriculture. Describe the emergence of civilization in Mesopotamia, Egypt, and the Indus valley. Discuss the importance of early technological innovations and of the ideas contributed by Hebrew and Greek civilizations. Describe the rise and fall of the Roman Empire.

Describe and date the rise of civilizations in China, India, and the Americas; the contributions of Islamic societies between 700 and 1400 A.D.; and the impact of the Mongol conquests. Discuss developments in Europe during the Dark and Middle Ages, the Renaissance, the Reformation, and the period of European expansion and colonization.

Describe the evolution of the idea of political rights in England; the importance of the ideas of the Enlightenment; contributions of the English, American, and French Revolutions; legal property rights and the rise of capitalism; the Industrial Revolution; and the rise of the labor movement and socialist ideas.

Discuss the causes and consequences of World War I, the Great Depression, and World War II. Describe events in the Soviet Union from October 1917 to the fall of the Communist Party in 1991. Explain Nazi ideology and its connection to the Holocaust; discuss other examples of attempted genocide in the twentieth century. Discuss the tension between ideas of democracy and universal human rights, on the one hand, and ethnic, national, and religious conflicts and divisions on the other.

Geography

Picking at random a country with a population of over five million, your child should be able to say where the country is located, its approximate level of economic development, and something about its climate and population density. Know about the location of important industries and patterns of world trade and be able to discuss the influence of geography on patterns of migration, political rivalries, or important historical events. Discuss factors that have influenced the location of industries, roads, and neighborhoods in her own community or region; use and interpret maps, charts, and geographic information systems; and describe in her own words what geography is about.

Civics and Government

Democracy and civil society. Define and discuss the importance of civic life, politics, and government. Describe advantages and disadvantages of several processes by which political decisions can be made. Explain the importance of minority rights in a system of majority rule.

Describe differences between limited and unlimited governments, giving specific examples of each; describe the distinction between authoritarian and totalitarian government; and discuss and debate the usefulness of that distinction. Compare and contrast the behavior of limited and unlimited governments in specific historical periods. For example, discuss how the policies and behavior of the U.S. government during the Great Depression and World War II differed from those of Nazi Germany and debate which Nazi policies could or would have been adopted and carried out had Germany been a democracy.

Political institutions. Discuss the nature and purposes of constitutions; parliamentary governments and systems of shared powers; federal and unitary systems; and winner-take-all systems versus those with proportional representation. Describe competing theories about the responsibilities of political representatives—to vote their conscience or represent the opinions of their constituents? Describe the responsibilities of the branches of government in the United States and the division of power and responsibility among federal, state, and local governments. Debate different theories about the responsibilities of government and the desirable extent of government regulation. Discuss the nature and role of international organizations.

Citizenship and public policy. Discuss factors that influence public opinion and that help to move an issue to the top of the public agenda. Discuss the role of political parties in the United States and other countries; describe how candidates are elected; and discuss processes by which public policies are adopted.

Discuss the rights and responsibilities of citizens; discuss and debate which behaviors, values, and attitudes contribute to the improvement of society; and describe opportunities to become involved in community activities and efforts to affect public policy.

Economics

Macroeconomics. Describe economists' ideas about how government fiscal and monetary policy work. Discuss examples of the use of these policies and debates over their effects on economic growth. Discuss and debate the positive and negative effects of specific government taxing and spending policies.

Discuss the trade-off between current and future consumption; the role of labor productivity and the distribution of income in influencing standards of living; and the role of human and physical capital and technology in increasing labor productivity. Describe what inflation is and distinguish between a change in relative prices and a rise in the overall price level. Distinguish between income and wealth and between nominal and real (adjusted for inflation) output. Describe one or more of the difficulties in measuring real income and real wealth. Discuss various causes of unemployment. Discuss and debate the relationship between income, wealth, and well-being.

Microeconomics. Discuss supply and demand: the relationship between the quantity supplied or demanded and relative prices and other factors. Discuss effects of price controls and supports and government subsidies. Describe effects of market competition on customer service and innovation. Discuss effects of organizing an industry as a monopoly or cartel. Discuss reasons for using markets or government to allocate income or make economic decisions. Describe examples of market and government failure.

International economics. Discuss patterns of international trade and theories of why industries locate where they do. Describe the effect of changes in exchange rates on import and export prices and the relationship between capital flows into a country and the country's trade deficit.

Society and Culture

Your high-schooler should be able to give examples of behaviors that differ across cultures and of other behaviors that are encouraged—or discouraged—in almost every culture. Discuss and debate the origin of values and of ideas of right and wrong, and the influence those ideas have on society. Describe ways that individual behavior makes societies livable or unlivable. Distinguish informal constraints on behavior imposed by peer groups from formal constraints imposed by laws and courts. Discuss good and bad influences that groups and institutions have on individuals' behavior, giving examples from current and past societies. Discuss social status and social class and ways that attempts to increase social status can have good or bad influences on individuals' behaviors.

Discuss the tendency to treat people as representative members of a group rather than as individuals. Describe factors that increase or decrease conflicts between individuals and groups. Describe the effects of these conflicts and discuss ways to resolve conflicts among individuals and groups.

Fine Arts

Your child should have an opportunity to participate in and appreciate the following art forms: painting, sculpture, instrumental music, opera, ballet, other forms of song and dance, and drama. Become proficient in communicating ideas and feelings through at least one art form. Improve her own artistic and musical performance and benefit from feedback given by others.

Be familiar with great works of art from different times and cultures, describe the historical period and style of these works, and discuss why the works are considered excellent.

Health and Fitness

Your high-school student should know different kinds of disease causes, such as bacteria, viruses, other microorganisms, harmful chemicals and radiation, heredity, old age, and allergic and autoimmune reactions. Describe the most common causes of disease and death in young and old adults. Identify risk factors for common diseases, discuss the relative strength of these risk factors and how they vary by age and sex, and describe some of the research used to identify risk factors. Identify behaviors that endanger one's own life and health and those of others. Know the risks of drug abuse and drug addiction. Identify health-care facilities and programs in the local community and discuss methods and the importance of preventive health care.

Participate in individual and team sports; become proficient in at least one sport; and develop endurance, muscular coordination, balance, strength, flexibility, and speed. Follow a training program to improve several of these attributes.

WHAT RESEARCH AND STUDY SKILLS SHOULD MY CHILD LEARN?

Research and study skills should be taught throughout your child's elementary, middle, and high-school career.

Research skills. By the end of elementary school, she should learn how to find information using dictionaries, thesauruses, encyclopedias, atlases, computer databases and the Internet, and various kinds of library reference books and indexes. In middle and high school, the number of sources of information with which she is familiar should increase every year. In addition, she should learn how to acquire information by interviewing experts on a subject.

Study skills. By the end of elementary school, she should learn how to distinguish more and less important ideas and concepts and give priority to understanding the most important ideas. She should be able to construct an "idea map," which shows relationships among the concepts that she has learned. She should be able to read passages for main ideas, take notes, and review her notes afterward. She should be able to distinguish more and less important ideas and information in her notes. In middle school, she should learn how to take notes when listening to others talk.

WHAT NONACADEMIC SKILLS SHOULD MY CHILD LEARN?

Academic skills are important, but your child's future success also depends on nonacademic skills. Some of these include

Workplace knowledge. She should understand the importance of showing up on time, completing tasks on schedule, and being helpful to customers and fellow workers. She should be able to see how the people in an organization depend on each other and how the success of some tasks depends on the successful completion of other tasks and on the efforts of her coworkers. She should learn how to work as an effective team leader or member on group projects.

Personal organization and time management. She should learn how to plan and work ahead so that long-term assignments can be completed on time. She should allow time to revise her work. She should learn how to set priorities when several things must be done and keep a calendar describing when tasks must be completed and when assignments are due.

Social skills. She should learn how to treat other people politely and fairly, listen respectfully to them and understand their point of view, and know ways to work with people whose social skills are not well developed.

Good habits and character. Her school should teach and encourage honesty, respect, and responsibility, which you also teach at home. She should understand the importance of hard work in producing success. She should develop skills in self-control, self-discipline, and self-motivation and the willingness to speak out and take action when something is wrong.

CHECKLIST: ACADEMIC STANDARDS

What You Need to Do	Source	Done
Get the school's curriculum for each grade and subject (content standards).	Teacher, principal	☐
Ask for examples of excellent, good, and satisfactory work in each subject and grade level (performance standards).	Teacher, principal	☐
Compare the school's standards with those in the best schools you can find and with nationally or internationally recognized standards.	Principal, appendix	☐
Find out how well "A" students perform on standardized tests and in higher grade levels, college, and work.	Principal	☐
Show work that meets the high school's standards to college educators and employers who pay high wages.	Job and college fairs	☐
Find out which courses are advanced/honors and enroll your child in those courses. Enroll her in preparatory or prerequisite courses first, if necessary.	School counselor	☐
Don't let her get placed in low-standards courses.		☐

What You Need to Do	Source	Done
Understand the difference between low-standards courses and courses designed to catch students up.		☐
If your child is enrolled in any courses or services for academically delayed students, find out when she will catch up and be prepared to take advanced or honors courses.	Teacher, counselor	☐
Learn about what your child should be learning at different ages and grade levels.	Teacher, appendix	☐

NOTES

1. For example, one study found that two-thirds of U.S. seventeen-year-olds could not place the Civil War within the correct half-century and fewer than 40 percent could identify the purpose of the Emancipation Proclamation. Another study found that only around half of high-school seniors have a firm grasp of seventh-grade mathematics, while only one in twenty had mastered problems from first-year algebra and geometry. Thirty-seven percent of high-school seniors did not know the meaning of "five percent" in the sentence "Five percent of the labor force is now unemployed." In a third study, only 36 percent of twelfth-graders could identify a rain forest from a description and name a country that has one. In a national assessment of students' best writing, only 12 percent of eighth-graders received high marks for narrative writing and only 4 percent got high marks for informative writing.

A nationwide study of the literacy of American adults found that 48 percent had difficulty writing a brief letter explaining an error on a credit card bill and 51 percent had trouble interpreting a simple bar graph. Another study found that only 20 percent of U.S. adults knew the purpose of DNA in heredity and half did not know how long it takes for the earth to go once around the sun.

See Diane Ravitch and Chester Finn, *What Do Our 17-Year-Olds Know?* (New York: Harper & Row, 1987), 49 and 62; Ina Mullis et al., *The State of Mathematics Achievement: Executive Summary*, 6–7; Ina Mullis, John Dossey, Eugene Owen, and Gary Phillips, *The State of Mathematics Achievement* (Washington, D.C.: National Center for Education Statistics, 1990), 70; Paul Williams, Clyde Reese, Stephen Lazer, and Sharif Shakrani, *NAEP 1994 Geography: A First Look* (Washington, D.C.: U.S. Department of Education, 1995), 58; Claudia Gentile, James Martin-Rehrmann, and John H. Kennedy, *Windows into the Classroom: NAEP's 1992 Writing Portfolio Study* (Washington, D.C.: U.S. Department of Education, 1995), 4; Irwin Kirsch, Ann Jungeblut, Lynn Jenkins, and Andrew Kolstad, *Adult Literacy in America: A First Look at the Results of the National Adult Literacy Survey* (Washington, D.C.: National Center for Education Statistics, 1993), 10 and 17; Science and Engineering Indicators: 1993 (Washington, D.C.: National Science Foundation), chap. 7. See also Lawrence Stedman, "Respecting the Evidence: The Achievement Crisis Remains Real," *Education Policy Analysis Archives* (1996), available on the Internet at http://olam.ed.asu.edu/epaa.

2. For the biology standards, see John S. Kendall and Robert J. Marzano, *Content Knowledge: A Compendium of Standards and Benchmarks for K–12 Education* (Aurora, Colo.: Mid-Continent Regional Educational Laboratory, 1996).

These important skills may be applied in different subject areas. For example, your child can do research, write, and give an oral presentation about a historical or scientific topic.

3. Most elementary schools don't teach about exponents (5²) or roots. This results in such incidents as the following: The child of a friend of the author's took the exam to enter sixth grade in a top local private school. He came home wondering about the "funny check marks" in the math section of the test. They were square root signs.

4. The answers to questions 5–9 are based on a review of the academic standards proposed by the following organizations:

American Association for the Advancement of Science
American Federation of Teachers
California Department of Education
Core Knowledge Foundation
Council on Basic Education
Delaware Department of Public Instruction
Edison Project
Hudson Institute, Modern Red Schoolhouse
Massachusetts Department of Education
Mid-Continent Regional Educational Laboratory
National Center for Civic Education
National Center for History in the Schools
National Council of Teachers of Mathematics
National Geographic Society
Saxon Publishers (Saxon Mathematics Program)
Texas Education Agency
Virginia Department of Education

5. Sound awareness is called "phonemic awareness" by researchers. Extensive research has shown that sound awareness is a critical skill for reading: good readers have it and poor readers do not.

6. Students whose reading instruction begins in kindergarten have better reading skills in high school. See Russell Gersten, "Long-Term Benefits from Direct Instruction," *Educational Leadership* (March 1987): 28–31; and Ralph Hanson and Donna Farrell, "The Long-Term Effects on High School Seniors of Learning to Read in Kindergarten," *Reading Research Quarterly* (October–December 1995): 908–33.

7. A common way of expressing this is to say that teaching knowledge and skills early is "not developmentally appropriate," which means "not appropriate for the child's age and stage." Remember that not teaching knowledge and skills to children who are ready and eager to learn them may also be inappropriate. See E. D. Hirsch, *The Schools We Need and Why We Don't Have Them* (New York: Doubleday, 1996), 79–83.

8. For example, a preschooler who counts past eighty and ninety may at first call one hundred "tenty."

9. A good discussion of the importance of specific reading skills—and the ages at which they should be learned—is in Bill Honig's book, *Teaching Our Children to Read: The Role of Skills in a Comprehensive Reading Program* (Thousand Oaks, Calif.: Corwin Press, 1996).

10. A good list of these books is in *Books to Build On: A Grade-by-Grade Resource Guide for Parents and Teachers,* John Holdren and E. D. Hirsch, eds. (New York: Doubleday, 1996).

11. A few encyclopedias, such as Britannica, are written for college-level readers. Encyclopedias that your fifth-grader should be able to read include *World Book, Microsoft Encarta, Compton's Encyclopedia,* and *The New Book of Knowledge.*

12. Joannie M. Schrof, "What Kids Will Have to Know," *U.S. News and World Report* (April 1, 1996): 57–60.

3

What Has Your Child Learned?

Assessments of student learning can be used to
A. find out what your child has learned
B. encourage your child to master challenging
material
C. compare your child's learning with that of
students in other schools
D. identify which schools are most effective
E. all of the above

QUESTIONS ADDRESSED IN THIS CHAPTER

- How is classroom assessment useful?
- How are external assessments useful?
- How can student learning be assessed?
- What are the strengths and weaknesses of different assessment methods?
- What is "teaching to the test," and when is it good or bad?
- What causes test score inflation?
- How can we make sure that assessments give a full picture of student learning?
- What do we know about assessment of young children (ages 5–7)?
- How should my child's learning be assessed?

Assessments are ways of finding out what a student has learned. They include pencil-and-paper tests, evaluations of samples of the student's work, student presentations, interviews with the student, and observations by the teacher. Your own observations of your child's work are also important; however, in this chapter, the focus is on assessments done by the school.

Classroom assessments are used by the teacher to keep track of your child's learning on a daily or weekly basis.

External assessments, such as standardized tests, compare student learning in different classrooms and schools.[1] External assessments are given once or twice a year—sometimes only once every several years—and provide a "second opinion" about your child's learning, to supplement the information that the teacher provides. They can compare his learning to standards for excellent performance from outside the school.

Assessments can be both an "alarm bell" to warn when your child isn't learning what he should and a "spotlight" to illuminate what is working in education and which schools are doing the best job.

HOW IS CLASSROOM ASSESSMENT USEFUL?

Good classroom assessment allows your child's teacher to

Provide information to you about what your child has learned. The teacher should be able to show you whether he is mastering a challenging academic curriculum, such as the one described in chapter 2, and show you his improvement over time.

Teach him what he does not already know. The teacher can identify where he needs extra help and where he has mastered the material and is ready to move ahead.

Identify teaching approaches that work well in the classroom and discard those that don't.

HOW ARE EXTERNAL ASSESSMENTS USEFUL?

They provide a backup for teacher-provided assessments. You and the teacher can benefit from a "second opinion" about your child's academic success. For some parents, a low test score is the first news they receive about their children's academic difficulties.

They can inform you about your school's academic strengths and weaknesses. For instance, if the school has had trouble in the past teaching fractions to fourth-graders, you can pay extra attention to your fourth-grader's progress in this area.

They can be used in school improvement planning. If the school wants to get all students caught up in reading, it would help to know how many students are how far behind. Classroom assessments can also be used for this purpose if their results are tabulated and reported schoolwide.

They can determine your child's eligibility for course credit, high-school graduation, or admission to college. Tests tied to particular subject matter can encourage him to study harder—as do college entrance exams in Europe and Japan and Advanced Placement and International Baccalaureate exams in the United States.

They can compare your child's learning with that of students in other schools. Is he learning as much as similar students in the best schools in your city, state, or nation?[2] If he's an "average" or "advanced" student, how does his performance compare with that of average or advanced students in other schools?

To allow valid comparisons, the schools should give the same tests. The test should also be scored consistently, so that two students who produce the same answer receive the same score. Perfect scoring consistency is not possible for tasks that must be scored by judges or raters, such as essays or oral presentations. But a high degree of consistency is possible from adequately trained raters if the scoring standards are clear.[3] (See "Why It's Important to Score External Assessments Consistently.")

They can compare the effectiveness of schools and programs. Which schools are most effective at getting students to learn? Which reading or mathematics programs work best?

To do this, assessments must provide before-and-after comparisons for each student—how much did the students improve over the last year? This is similar to evaluating a weight-loss program by comparing each participant's weight *before* and *after* she participated in the program. (For more on school comparisons, see chapter 4.)

> Watch out for the misuse of test scores. Do teachers lower
> the academic standards for your child if he gets a low score?
> Do administrators use tests mainly for public relations
> purposes—sending the message that everything is fine
> as long as this year's scores are higher than last?[4]

WHY IT'S IMPORTANT TO SCORE EXTERNAL ASSESSMENTS CONSISTENTLY

If scoring is inconsistent, some students may be graded using a lower standard. Three researchers decided to investigate whether untrained raters would be able to score students' essays fairly. They gave sixty teachers an essay that began

> The happiest time that I had with my friends was when we went roller skating. Hectors mom drove us in the truck and it took a long time to get there because it was off the reservation. It was okay because we rode in the back. . . .

A second group of sixty teachers received a nearly identical essay that began

> The happiest time that I had with my friends was when we went roller skating. Henrys mom drove us and it took a long time to get down town. It was okay because she had this new BMW. . . .

The essay that earned the higher marks was . . . the pickup truck essay! Raters scored this essay almost a full point higher on a four-point scale—in effect giving the pickup truck writer a B and the BMW writer a C. The raters may have unconsciously applied a lower academic standard to the pickup truck writer, thinking, "This is a pretty good essay . . . for this kind of student," while those grading the BMW essay thought, "This student can do better than that!"[5]

HOW CAN STUDENT LEARNING BE ASSESSED?

Four of the common methods of assessing student learning are "on-demand," which means that the test writer supplies the questions and the student supplies the answers.

Multiple-choice tests. The student must select one best answer from a set of possible answers printed on the page. Most standardized tests are multiple choice because those tests can be scored easily and cheaply by computer.

Constructed-response tests. The student is asked questions that require written answers, or responses he must construct. He may be asked to write an essay, draw a diagram, or solve a math problem and show his work.

Performance tasks. The student is asked to do a task that does not involve pencil and paper, such as performing a science experiment, finding information on the Internet, or driving a car.

Oral interview tests. The student is asked questions by an examiner and must give the answers orally, rather than in writing. This is a common way to test young children—and graduate students.

Three common assessment methods allow the student to choose how to demonstrate his knowledge and skill.

Portfolios and work samples. These are samples of the student's work. Portfolios usually represent his *best* work, while work samples represent his *typical* work. (See "What You Can Learn from Portfolio Assessment.")

Projects. Rather than choosing samples of his everyday work, he does a special project, such as a science or art project, to demonstrate his skill.

Rehearsed presentations. The student gives a presentation in front of an audience, such as a speech, a narrated slide show, or an artistic or musical performance. He has an opportunity to practice for the performance.

Finally, **one method of assessment is not a test at all** but is very important in the classroom.

Informal teacher observations. The teacher observes the student on a daily basis and keeps track of what he can and cannot do.

WHAT YOU CAN LEARN FROM PORTFOLIO ASSESSMENT

Portfolio assessment can help you make three comparisons:

- Comparisons of your child's work to his own previous work. This lets you see his rate of progress.
- Comparisons of his work to papers showing your school's standards for excellent, good, or acceptable performance. These example papers—which may be created by teachers or students—should be public documents, available in every school to any parent who wants to see them.
- Comparisons of his work to an outside standard—papers representing standards for excellent performance in several of the best schools. These comparisons can let you know if your child's rate of progress needs to increase.

WHAT ARE THE STRENGTHS AND WEAKNESSES OF DIFFERENT ASSESSMENT METHODS?

Each method in the assessment toolbox is more useful for some purposes and less useful for others. It's important to use a variety of assessments for different purposes: "If all you have is a hammer, every problem looks like a nail."

Consistent scoring is much easier for on-demand assessments because all students respond to the same test questions. Tests scored by computer, such as multiple-choice tests, are graded with perfect consistency. However, on-demand assessments are not suitable for assessing certain types of skills, such as the ability to carry out a complex project over time.

For external assessments, cost and consistent scoring are important. This is why these assessments often rely heavily on multiple-choice questions, which can be scored by computer at a fraction of the cost of grading an essay or portfolio. Experiments are underway to figure out how to grade portfolios and projects consistently. However, consistent scoring of these will probably never be cheap, so if we want more comprehensive assessments, we had better be prepared to pay for them.[6]

Portfolios and projects may be subject to the question "Whose work is it?" when students receive help on their projects. Outside help can be a major problem in external assessment but is a minor issue in classroom assessment, since the classroom teacher is likely to have a good idea of how much help the student received.[7]

Portfolios, projects, rehearsed presentations, and teacher observations are useful for assessing "unanticipated learning"—learning that is not in the planned curriculum. In a good school, students are likely to become excited about learning, and they acquire knowledge and skills that curriculum planners and test designers do not anticipate.

WHAT IS "TEACHING TO THE TEST," AND WHEN IS IT GOOD OR BAD?

"Teaching to the test" is good when it means "preparing students to do well on the test by teaching the subject." If students must know the subject well in order to do well on the test, then teaching the subject is a good way to prepare students. Jaime Escalante was able to get a record number of low-income Hispanic high-school students to master calculus by teaching them the subject and challenging them to pass the Advanced Placement calculus test.

The more challenging the test, the more the test is "worth teaching to." Escalante's students had to develop a high level of mathematical skill in order to do well on the test.

Teaching to the test is bad when it means "teaching students only a few things so that they'll pass the test." This can happen when the test is too easy and when

Schools don't teach the subjects that aren't tested. For example, if external assessments cover mathematics but not science, history, or the fine arts, schools may neglect the teaching of science, history, and the fine arts.

Teachers cover only the types of tasks that are on the test, such as answering multiple-choice test questions or assembling a portfolio that meets only minimum specifications. The most extreme form of teaching to the test would, of course, be teaching students to answer the specific questions that are on the test.

Questions to ask: Is the school preparing students for tests by teaching them *more* or by teaching them *less?* Is the school preparing my child to do well on only *one* particular test? Or is the school preparing my child to do well on *any* test that covers material the students should know? Does the school understand that, if the students have strong skills and knowledge, the test scores will take care of themselves?

> Do educators in your local school or school district act as
> if their main mission is to raise test scores—no matter how?
> Or do they understand that their job is to promote student
> learning, which will lead to higher test scores?

WHAT CAUSES TEST SCORE INFLATION?

When test scores exaggerate how much the students know, that's test score inflation.[8] For example, high scores in reading and mathematics might hide the fact that the students know little about history, geography, science, or art. High scores on a multiple-choice test might hide an inability to do tasks that can't be examined by that test.

Test score inflation frustrates our ability to use assessments as an "alarm bell" to warn when our children aren't learning enough.

The Lake Wobegon Effect—in which all fifty states reported that their students scored above the national average on standardized tests—provided evidence that test score inflation is a widespread problem. A West Virginia physician, John Jacob Cannell, discovered the Lake Wobegon Effect after he began to investigate why students in his local school district who knew so little had acceptable scores on the district's standardized test.[9]

What causes test score inflation?

Some school districts give the exact same test year after year, so that teachers learn what is on the test and can get their students to do better every year. One Maryland school district gave the exact same test for ten years straight.[10]

The test may cover only a small but predictable part of the curriculum. This encourages teachers and students to focus narrowly on that part and ignore the rest. For this reason, when school systems use only *one* assessment method or type of question, they are vulnerable to test score inflation-especially if that single assessment method is the main way by which teachers and schools are evaluated (see chapter 10 on accountability systems).

The test can be made easier so that more students will pass. When 60 percent of Michigan students failed a science test in 1986, the state board of education decided that the problem was ... the test! They replaced it with an easier test in 1988. A coauthor of another test complained that school districts "have forced us not to have anything that's too difficult on the tests. For a superintendent, the criterion is often, 'Give me a test that makes me look good.'"[11]

The school may exempt many low-performing students from taking the test. We discuss this problem in chapter 4.

Check for test score inflation. Your state or district should give some students a second "audit test" covering the same subject matter-but that gives educators little incentive to inflate scores. If scores on the original test go up but those on the audit test do not, then we suspect that scores on the first test are inflated. Exactly this happened in Kentucky when scores on the state assessment rose between 1992 and 1994, while scores on the National Assessment of Educational Progress (NAEP) did not.[12]

Accurate information on how students and schools are doing is essential for parents, educators, and community leaders.

HOW CAN WE MAKE SURE THAT ASSESSMENTS GIVE A FULL PICTURE OF STUDENT LEARNING?

More than one assessment method should be used since each assessment method has its limitations. Different skills are best assessed in different ways: you wouldn't use the same method to assess a student's ability to paint a picture, solve a math problem, or give a talk to an audience. Using different assessment methods can also reduce test score inflation, making it difficult to raise scores by training students to do well on a narrow range of tasks.

The best tests use more than one method. Advanced Placement tests have essay and multiple-choice sections; the National Assessment of Educational Progress uses essays, multiple-choice, and performance tasks; and the International Baccalaureate uses essays, portfolios, and oral presentations.

> Your school should use several methods to assess your child's learning. Find out how they assess him in each subject.

The assessments as a group should cover the curriculum. The school should be able to document your child's learning in each subject area. The assessments should sound the alarm if any important part of the curriculum is being neglected in the classroom.

When the external assessments needed to cover the curriculum become long and complex, a common solution is to break up the assessment into parts and give each student part of the test. This approach provides good information about the school's success but only a partial picture of what your own child has learned.[13] If your school uses this approach, you can still use the test to learn whether your child's grades are a good success indicator: ask the school to provide information on how well the A students did on the exam (see chapter 4).

The assessments should be accurate, of course. Assessment experts use three measures of accuracy:

- **Validity:** Does the assessment measure what it is supposed to? Does the reading test measure how well students can read?
- **Reliability:** Does the assessment give consistent results when the same student is assessed twice?
- **Lack of bias:** Is the individual's test score influenced by irrelevant personal characteristics, such as race, sex, appearance, or handwriting neatness?

If individuals from a minority ethnic group do worse on a test, this is *not* by itself evidence that the test is biased. The minority students may have received a poor education and the test may be revealing that fact. The question is: do minority students *with the same level of academic skill* do worse on the test?

The assessments should reflect high academic standards. See whether students who do well on the assessment also do well on tests that are internationally recognized as having high standards: Advanced Placement tests, the International Baccalaureate exams, and the National Assessment of Educational Progress.

For example, although 69 percent of Texas eighth-grade students passed the state mathematics test in 1996, only 21 percent were mathematically "proficient" according to NAEP. In Georgia, 83 percent of eighth-graders were "adequate and acceptable" and 40 percent were "excellent" on the state test, while only 15 percent were proficient according to NAEP.[14]

Advanced Placement and International Baccalaureate tests are given at the high-school level. NAEP is given in grades 4, 8, and 12 to a sample of students in each state—none of whom take the entire test—and does not supply information on individual students, schools, or school districts. This increases NAEP's usefulness as an audit test to check for test score inflation, since no one has an incentive to inflate the NAEP scores.

However, this also leaves many parents without a good way to get a second opinion on their children's education. Proposals to create nationwide Advanced Placement-quality tests in grades 4 and 8 that parents could use for information on their own children and schools have faced stiff opposition.[15]

WHAT DO WE KNOW ABOUT ASSESSMENT OF YOUNG CHILDREN (AGES 5–7)?

Good assessment is important for young children. Children must get off to a good start, especially in reading, and prereading skills are important for very young children. You need to know whether your child is getting these skills and whether the school has difficulty teaching them to large numbers of students.

Good assessment is more difficult with young children. Young children have trouble concentrating and following directions. Some young children are shy and do not speak up well in oral interviews.

It's important to know what to assess. Assess skills that are important for children of that age to learn. Thus, an assessment of six-year-olds might focus on prereading and early reading skills.

It's important to look at patterns in groups of children. Individual children vary naturally in height and weight, but if all children in a group are unusually short and thin, you can suspect malnutrition. Likewise, some children are "late bloomers," but if the whole group is academically delayed, then something may be wrong with their education.

HOW SHOULD MY CHILD'S LEARNING BE ASSESSED?

Teachers at the school should

Assess your child carefully at the beginning and end of each school year—at the beginning so that the teacher knows what he needs to be taught, and at the end to see how much progress he has made.

Use classroom assessment throughout the year to provide quick, up-to-date information on your child. If he starts to fall behind, you and the teacher need to know about it quickly.

Use external assessment to see how his knowledge and skill measure up against outside standards.

Use more than one assessment method to get a complete picture of his learning. Teachers can select from multiple-choice and constructed-response tests, performance tasks, oral interviews, portfolios, projects, presentations, and their own observations.

Decisions to place your child in a special program
should be based on more than one assessment.

Assess your child at the level at which he actually works. If your third-grader is doing fifth-grade work, he should be able to take a fifth-grade test. A third-grade test will give less information about his academic level and progress.

The teacher should clearly explain the results of these assessments to you. Keep asking questions until you understand them.

CHECKLIST: ASSESSMENT OF STUDENT LEARNING

What You Need to Do	Source	Done
Learn about the purposes of classroom and external assessments.		☐
Learn how classroom and external assessments are different.		☐
Find out what external assessments your child will be given and how the results will be used.	Teacher, counselor	☐
Be sure he is given the same external assessments as other students, even if he could be exempted.	Principal, district office	☐
Find out what classroom and external assessments say about his strengths and weaknesses.	Teacher	☐
Find out what external assessments say about the school's strengths and weaknesses.	Teacher, principal	☐
Find out what assessments are used.	Teacher	☐
Find out how well classroom and external assessments cover the curriculum.	Teacher, principal	☐

What You Need to Do	Source	Done
Find out what your state or school district does to guard against test score inflation.	Principal, district office	☐
Find out which classroom and external assessments allow before-and-after comparisons so that student gain or progress can be measured.	Teacher, principal	☐
Find out how the school uses assessment information in its school improvement planning process.	Teacher, principal	☐

NOTES

1. External assessments are sometimes called large-scale assessments because they are given to large numbers of students in different schools.

2. External assessments could also be used to compare your child's learning with students in other countries, such as France and Japan. However, no one provides assessments that will give you this information. Existing international comparisons have been made using tests that do not report scores for individual students, because each student takes only part of the test.

3. Because of different tests and scoring inconsistency, student grades cannot be used to compare student learning in separate classrooms—an A given by one teacher may mean something different from an A given by a different teacher. Paul G. LeMahieu, Drew Gitomer, and JoAnne Eresh, "Portfolios in Large-Scale Assessment: Difficult but Not Impossible," *Educational Measurement: Issues and Practice* (Fall 1995): 11-16, 25-28.

4. Administrators should report something like, "Here's what our goals are, here's where we are today, here's the progress we've made so far, and here's how far we still have to go." Emphasizing where the district stands relative to ambitious academic goals can help prevent complacency.

5. Kenneth Howell, Susan Bigelow, and Ange Evoy, "A Qualitative Examination of an Authentic Assessment" (Western Washington University, Bellingham, 1993). This fits the pattern we saw in chapter 1 of low-income students' being held to a lower academic standard.

6. LeMahieu et al., "Portfolios in Large-Scale Assessment," 11-16, 25-28.

7. Helping the students may be just what is needed for good instruction, while good external assessment requires strict controls on the amount of outside help. Thus, the statement made by some educators that "good assessment is good instruction" is not necessarily true. See the discussion in Daniel Koretz, "Sometimes a Cigar Is Only a Cigar, and Often a Test Is Only a Test," in Diane Ravitch, ed., *Debating the Future of American Education* (Washington, D.C.: Brookings Institution, 1995), 154-66.

8. If test score inflation could be prevented, then the only way to produce high test scores would be to generate the desired high level of student learning. In that case, "teaching to the test" would not be an issue.

9. John J. Cannell, "Nationally Normed Elementary Achievement Testing in America's Public Schools: How All 50 States Are Above the National Average," *Educational Measurement: Issues and Practice* (Summer 1988): 5-9. The Lake Wobegon Effect is named after the imaginary Minnesota town in stories by Gar-

rison Keillor, in which "all the children are above average." For a more complete discussion of the Lake Wobegon Effect, see Chester E. Finn, *We Must Take Charge: Our Schools and Our Future* (New York: Free Press, 1991).

10. Thomas Toch, *In the Name of Excellence* (New York: Oxford University Press, 1991), 222.

11. Toch, *In the Name of Excellence*, 211.

12. Ronald K. Hambleton et al., *Review of the Measurement Quality of the Kentucky Instructional Results Information System, 1991-94: Final Report* (Lexington: Office of Educational Accountability, Kentucky General Assembly, June 1995), 8.8-8.11. This study also concluded that Kentucky's assessment should include multiple-choice questions as well as essays and performance tasks and that more effort was needed to find ways to score the students' portfolios consistently. Omitting multiple-choice and short-answer questions limited the number of test questions and the variety of topics covered.

13. This approach is called matrix sampling.

14. The Texas 8th grade passing rule of 69% n the state test was closer to the 59% of Texas 8th graders who met or exceeded the NAEP "basic" standard, which reflects "partial mastery" of grade level material. Mark Musick, "You Can't Catch up in Education by Setting Low Standards," *Network News and Views* (June 1996): 48-51. NAEP began in 1971 as an assessment of educational progress of the nation as a whole. Periodic assessment of student learning by state began in 1990.

15. See Chester Finn, "Who's Afraid of the Big, Bad Test?," in Diane Ravitch, ed., *Debating the Future of American Education* (Washington, D.C.: Brookings Institution, 1995), 120-44. Another issue is how to motivate students to do their best work on an audit test, such as NAEP.

4

How Good Are Your Local Schools?

Is the drinking water or something different over here?
You can't tell me that the kids over here are any differ-
ent than the kids anywhere else....We thought they did
pretty well.

— *Texas parent, after learning that more than*
80 percent of the fourth-grade students in
eight local schools had failed the state
test in reading, writing, or mathematics

QUESTIONS ADDRESSED IN THIS CHAPTER

- What do successful schools accomplish?
- What should I look for when I visit a school?
- What are my school's priorities, programs, and plans?
- How can I compare schools?
- How good are my school's academic results?
- How can published school information mislead us?
- What can I do if important school information is not available?
- How can I get an independent professional evaluation of my child's school?
- What choices are available if I need to change schools?

Teachers have no control over what students know when they enter school. But teachers can do something about the progress they make. How much more do students know now compared to when they started? To evaluate a school, look at what the school adds to what the students already know—and take into account the extra effort needed to reach some students.

Good information on how much knowledge students have gained can be hard to come by, since it requires giving before-and-after assessments to the same students, as we saw in chapter 3. If enough people want this information and ask for it, we can end the "data drought."[1]

WHAT DO SUCCESSFUL SCHOOLS ACCOMPLISH?

Successful schools

Teach the basics of reading, writing, mathematics, science, history, geography, and the fine arts.

Introduce students to the best of human knowledge and culture.

Provide an academically challenging education for all students—students who start out ahead, who are average, or who start out behind.

Encourage good work habits and an enthusiasm for learning.

Provide a safe and orderly environment for learning and encourage values of honesty, responsibility, and respect.

See chapter 2 for more on what successful schools accomplish.

WHAT SHOULD I LOOK FOR WHEN I VISIT A SCHOOL?

There is no better way to learn about a school than to spend time there yourself during the school day. This applies to the school your child attends and any school where you may be thinking of enrolling her.

Before you visit a school for the first time, ask the principal to send you any published information on the school: class sizes, test scores, and programs offered. Study this information before you visit the school.

Talk to any parents you know who have or have had children attend the school. Ask them about the school's specific strengths and weaknesses. What do they most like about the school? What do they least like? Has the school changed in any important ways since they first enrolled their children there? Has the school encouraged them to get involved?

Visit as many classrooms as you can. This enables you to get a good sample of the teaching styles and classroom management available at a school. Do the teachers appear to be enthusiastic about teaching and learning? Do they seem to know the subjects they are teaching? Do they present ideas clearly? Do teachers and students act as if they're glad to see each other?

If you can, show up when the students first arrive at school and observe their manner and behavior when they walk into the building. Does anyone from the school greet them and treat them as if they are welcome? Do many students straggle in late?

Ask about the school's visitor policy. Some schools are concerned that too many visitors will disrupt classes; they may require setting up appointments ahead of time.

Take a look at the physical state of the school. What is the appearance of the building? Is it neat and clean? Are the bathrooms in good repair? Is this a place where *you* would want to go to school? Is a variety of students' work in multiple subjects displayed on the walls?

Look at the students and their work. In the classrooms, are the students doing their work or do they seem bored or distracted? Do they seem to understand what they are supposed to be doing? Look at displays of the students' work in classrooms and hallways. Do the assignments and activities seem to be appropriate for the age and grade of the students? Are the students given challenging and interesting work? Are they encouraged to do special projects where they can pursue their interests in depth?

Look at the school's expectations of its students. Are students expected to learn the basic skills? Are they encouraged to read? Do the books that they read appear to be too easy for their grade level? Are they expected to write coherently and spell and use grammar correctly? Is there evidence that they are learning how to compute and to reason mathematically? Are students encouraged to think and reason as well as to memorize?

Talk to the principal and teachers. If you have any questions, make arrangements to address them to the principal at a time when he can give you his undivided attention. You should also make appointments to talk to two or three teachers at a time when class is not in session.

Talk to the school counselor about the services available for the students. Ask how you can enroll your child in advanced courses. Find out what extracurricular activities are available and whether the school requires good academic standing for participation.

Visit the school library. Find out how many books were checked out last year, what kinds of special services and equipment are available, and how much money is spent annually for new books and subscriptions.

Find out about students' access to current technology and course materials. How current are the students' textbooks? Do the geography textbooks still show the Soviet Union, or do they show Russia and the other independent republics? Do students have access to computers for word processing, graphics, database applications, and spreadsheets? How often do they get to use them? Do they have access to the Internet?

VISIT THE BEST SCHOOLS

If you learn about other schools that are doing an excellent job, pay them a visit. Encourage other parents, teachers, and administrators to visit them as well. It's important to visit more than one excellent school, since not all schools use the same methods to achieve excellence.

Even if your own school is one of the best schools, you can still learn from visiting other schools. Those schools may have strengths in different areas: one may have an outstanding history program, while another may be unusually good in teaching math or science.

WHAT ARE MY SCHOOL'S PRIORITIES, PROGRAMS, AND PLANS?

Priorities

Look for priorities that focus on student learning:

Does the school stress the importance of learning? Does the school challenge every student academically-students who start out ahead, in the middle, or behind? Does the school have high academic standards? (See chapter 2.) Do the school's academic stars get recognition similar to that of the athletic stars?

Does the school's budget reflect a priority of learning? One West Texas high school spent more money to speed up the processing of football films so that they could be watched on Saturday rather than Monday than it did on instructional materials for its entire English department.[2]

Does the school stress safety, order, and values? Do the students feel safe? Does the school encourage values of honesty, responsibility, and respect among students and teachers? Does the school encourage good study habits and attitudes toward learning?

What are the school's specific priorities for improving itself? Examples of school improvement priorities might be:

- An elementary school makes sure that every student can read fourth-grade material by the time she begins the fourth grade.
- A middle school develops after-school activities that keep students out of gangs.
- A high school develops a first-rate history program.

Too many priorities can mean no priorities.

Programs

Look for programs that are student-oriented and accomplish the following goals:[3]

Encourage students to learn as rapidly as they can. Students who are academically delayed must be identified early and not be allowed to fall further behind. The school should find programs that motivate students who have become "turned off" to school. Every school should have a gifted and talented program that encourages academically advanced students to move ahead at their own pace.

Teach second languages to students. It's important that students become truly proficient in more than one language. The best time to begin second-language training is as early as possible, preferably in preschool or kindergarten.

Provide extracurricular and after-school programs that are not limited to sports. The school should provide academic and artistic programs, such as a science club, a drama club, or a school newspaper. Look for such school events as an art show, book fair, spelling bee, geography bee, mathematics competition, or science fair.

Involve parents and the community. Parents, teachers, and community leaders should work together to help students learn. (For ideas on how to make this happen, see chapter 11.)

Schools must be willing to drop less effective programs in favor of more effective ones.

> Look out for programs that cost a lot of money and are
> popular but don't accomplish much. Your school district
> should evaluate each program: Does the program have specific
> goals? Does it accomplish these goals? Are there other
> programs that could accomplish more for the same cost?

Plans

Does the school have real plans or only paper plans? Many schools have a "school improvement plan" or "campus improvement plan" that is available to the public. In some cases these are taken seriously, while in other cases the plans are created to satisfy school district requirements and are otherwise ignored. How can you tell the difference? Real plans

Identify specific and measurable goals. For example, the goal "We want to make sure that all students can read" is too vague. *How well* should the students read? The goal that "every student from second grade on should be able to read material designed for that child's grade" is more specific and desirable.

Describe how to measure whether you have reached the goals. For example, the school might use pencil-and-paper tests, oral interview assessments, and records of the students reading aloud to determine how well each child can read.

List specific steps required to get to each goal. Which steps are likely to produce the required improvement in the students' reading levels? Who is responsible for making sure the steps are taken?

Use past experience to identify what will work. If there is no basis in past experience to believe that the proposed steps will lead to the attainment of the goal, then the document is a wish and not a plan.

Contain estimates of the cost and time required to reach the goals. What resources are required to achieve the goals? Where will these resources come from? What will be accomplished by what dates?

Are carried out, not just filed away and forgotten until the next plan is due. Therefore, you may ask teachers and the principal if they are familiar with the plan and what is being done to carry it out. Do they have a record of whether previous years' plans were carried out and what those plans accomplished? When will the success of the current plan be reviewed? Will parents and teachers be part of the review?

Accomplish the desired goals, or are changed if they don't.

Campus improvement plans should be readily available to the public. Find out how you can get a copy of the plan. Is it available to everyone? Is the plan written in language that you can understand? Does your child's teacher have a copy?

See chapter 11 on how to get involved in your school's improvement planning process.

HOW CAN I COMPARE SCHOOLS?

Comparing schools can enable you to answer the following questions:

Which schools offer the best education available? If students who resemble your child are doing better somewhere else, your child probably should be learning more. You can learn whether to expect more from her current school—or consider moving her to a different school.

Which schools are the best at teaching each academic subject? If the history program is much stronger somewhere else, you can ask your child's teacher to help you find books or other resources to help her learn the missing information. If possible, look for ways to contribute the missing books to the classroom or school library.

Which schools are best at working with students who resemble your child? Some schools work better with advanced or gifted students; others work better with students who have fallen behind; still others with students with specific talents, such as art or mathematics.

Which schools are strong where your child's school is weak? You can use this information to investigate possibilities for improvement in your school. Your teacher and principal can use this information too. If the fourth-grade teachers are weak in teaching fractions, they can learn from other teachers who are strong in this area. If these same teachers do an excellent job of teaching writing, then teachers in other schools can learn from them.

> Be careful when making comparisons between schools.
> Be sure you're comparing "apples to apples." (See below.)

When making comparisons, be sure to do the following:[4]

Look at student progress or *academic gains*, not just levels of performance. Gains are what matter when evaluating how well a school is doing. How much more do the students know in May than they did in September? Look at figure 1. Is Jones or Smith the better school? The average sixth-grade student in Smith finished the year at a seventh-grade reading level, while the average student at Jones finished at a sixth-grade level. Smith appears to be better. But look again. Jones students began the year reading on a third-grade level and made three years' progress in a single year—Smith students, only one year's progress. On a second look, Jones clearly has a better sixth-grade reading program.

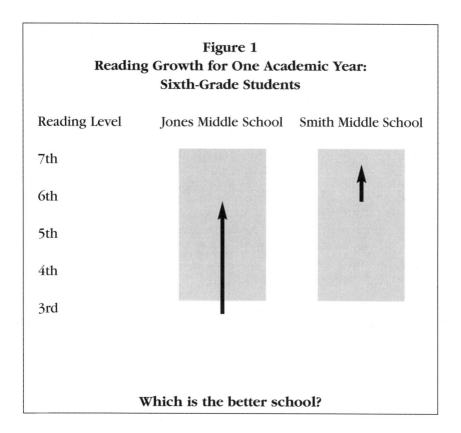

Figure 1
Reading Growth for One Academic Year:
Sixth-Grade Students

Reading Level   Jones Middle School   Smith Middle School

7th

6th

5th

4th

3rd

Which is the better school?

If your child starts out behind, she will need to make more than a year's academic progress every year. Find out how the school identifies students who aren't making enough progress, what it does to help those students, and how effective that help is. Do other schools have better programs for these students?

Look at several years' information. Does the sixth grade at Jones Middle School do a good job year after year?

Compare how schools do with similar students. Do advanced students gain more at this school than at other schools? What about average students, or students who start out behind? Is the school good at working with low-income students, or students who come to school knowing little English?

Some magnet or private schools admit only the best students.
When comparing these schools with other schools, it's
especially important to remember this rule: *compare
academic gains by similar groups of students.*

Take into account the extra effort needed to reach some students, while keeping standards high for all students. In Olympic diving, the judges award more points for a difficult dive done well. Easy dives receive fewer points. Likewise, a school that succeeds with students that other schools find hard to teach has accomplished a more difficult job. Teachers of hard-to-teach students should be given extra resources and incentives to do their job.[5]

Look at how all of the students are doing. Many schools exclude some of their academically behind students from standardized testing. Of course, this makes the school appear to be doing a better job. A weight-loss program that counted only participants who lost the most weight, or a hospital that counted only its healthiest patients, would look very effective!

Find out if your school excludes any students
from schoolwide testing. Does the school exempt
more than two or three percent of the students?

Take into account how long students have been enrolled in the school. If a fourth-grader who entered the school two weeks ago can't read, that's little reflection on the accomplishments of the school. However, if the same student can't read after she has been in the same school since kindergarten, then the school must bear responsibility for that failure. (See chapter 10 on accountability.)

HOW GOOD ARE MY SCHOOL'S ACADEMIC RESULTS?

Look for these kinds of information:

- scores on tests and assessments
- enrollment in advanced courses

- academic awards
- examples of student work
- graduation rates
- student success after graduation
- surveys of parents, students, teachers, and employers

When you want information about the school in which your child is enrolled, ask the teacher to direct you to the right source. When inquiring about other schools, contact your principal, the school district's central office, or the other schools directly.

Scores on Tests and Assessments

Assessments can include pencil-and-paper tests, oral interviews, and samples of the students' classroom work (see chapter 3). If assessments are to be used to compare schools, *they should be scored consistently*: for example, a score of 4 on a student's essay should reflect the same level of performance as a 4 received by another student in a different school. Here's what we can do with assessment information:

Look at academic gains for different groups of students—students who start out ahead, who are average, and who start out behind. One school may be best at working with advanced students, another at catching up academically delayed students, a third at working with average students. Does the school do a good job of challenging nearly all of the students who are ahead, or just a few of them? Does the school do a good job catching up nearly all of the students who are behind, or just a few of them?

Compare students' grades and test scores. Do the elementary and middle schools' A students consistently do well on the state's or school district's standardized tests? Do the high schools' A students consistently do well on academically challenging exams from outside the school, such as Advanced Placement tests or the International Baccalaureate exams?

Compare student scores on different kinds of assessments. If students do well answering multiple-choice test questions, can they also write a clear paragraph? If their classroom portfolios look good, can they also do a good job of explaining what is in them, explaining what makes their contents important, and describing how much help they received on them?

Look at the school's performance in specific grades and subject areas. One school may be best in mathematics, another in writing; one elementary school may be stronger in first and second grade, while another school may be better in third and fourth grade.

Get information on test score levels and gains by students who have been at the school for more than two years. This way we can see how students do when the school's program has been given time to work.

Student Enrollment in Advanced Courses

Ask these questions about your child's middle or high school:

What percent of students pass first-year algebra by the end of eighth grade? What percent of students are enrolled in mathematics courses beyond first-year algebra?

How many students take advanced courses in science, history, and literature every semester? Does the school encourage students to sign up for these courses? Is the school able to get students from high-poverty backgrounds to do well in these courses?

> Some courses labeled "advanced," "honors," or "college preparatory" don't live up to their labels, so make sure the courses in your school do. See chapter 1.

How many high-school students are enrolled in Advanced Placement courses in each subject? These students are able to earn college credit if they pass the Advanced Placement exam in that subject at the end of the course. How many of the school's students take and pass these exams in each subject?

> Does every high school in the district offer Advanced Placement courses? If they don't, why not?

Does the high school offer the International Baccalaureate program? This program gives students an internationally recognized set of courses followed by exams that are graded outside the school. (See the appendix for where to go for additional information.) How many students are enrolled and how many earn the International Baccalaureate degree?

Academic Awards

Look at awards that show evidence of academic success.

Student success in academic competitions. There are dozens of academic contests and exhibitions every year—spelling bees, mathematics contests, science fairs, essay contests, debate tournaments, art shows, and so on. A contest has only one winner or winning team per event, while an exhibition, such as a science fair, can recognize anyone whose work meets standards for excellent work.

The best scholastic events provide clear feedback to students on the quality of their work, encourage interest in excellence in the subject matter rather than simply "beating" someone else, and encourage students to present their work to audiences outside the school.[6]

Does the school enter students in these events? If not, why not? (Most high schools have no trouble fielding a football team every year.) If so, how many events does the school enter, how many students participate, and how many prize-winning entries do they produce?

Scholarships earned by students. Many colleges, universities, and private donors award merit scholarships to students who show particular promise. How many of these scholarships do the school's students earn?

Exemplary school recognition. Some states and school districts offer money and recognition to the more successful schools. Find out from your state education agency or local school district what schools have to do to earn these awards.

Examples of Students' Work

Places where you can see the students' work on public display include:

- displays in the classrooms and hallways
- student entries in science fairs, art shows, and other competitions
- a school newspaper or creative writing yearbook
- school plays
- student talks and debates
- collections of student work kept by the school and made available to the public

It's important to look at a wide variety of student work—you don't want to base your impression of the school on the accomplishments of a few students. Do *all* of the students produce work for some kind of public display? If you can see the work of only a few top students, that's like seeing average test scores only for the top students.

Graduation Rates

There are many ways to calculate graduation rates, but the main one you need to know is this: **What percent of students who enter the ninth grade for the first time graduate four years later? How many of those students graduate within five years?**[7]

Unfortunately, these are not the calculated graduation rates you are likely to see. Some school districts only report the graduation rate of students who entered the twelfth grade. Since most failing students have dropped out by that time, the twelfth-grade graduation rates are usually high.

The graduation rate of entering ninth-graders four or five years later usually can't be calculated from the annual dropout rates that school districts report. If a student repeats the ninth grade for four years, for example, that student will not be reported as a dropout, but she will not graduate. Also, students may advance to the twelfth grade and then fail to pass a state minimum skills test for graduation.

Student Success after Graduation

Most private schools keep track of their graduates, while most public schools do not. That is because private schools actively raise money from their alumni—an idea that public schools might consider.[8]

You may want to know:

How well do the graduates of your child's elementary school do in middle school and how well do the graduates of her middle school do in high school? If the school district does not keep this information, go to the middle school or high school and ask teachers how academically well prepared the students from your child's school are.

How many graduates from your child's high school go on to college? How many are accepted by selective colleges (colleges that reject many of the applicants who apply)? How many graduate from community college, technical school, or four-year college?

How many graduates from your child's high school have to take remedial courses in college? Several states are beginning to collect this information.

How many students who graduate without going on to college have a steady job six months later? Find out if your state has plans to collect this information.

Surveys of Parents, Teachers, Students, and Employers

Surveys can provide answers to questions that can't easily be answered by numbers:

- Has the school contributed to your child's intellectual curiosity and eagerness to learn?
- Has the school encouraged good study habits and values in your child?
- Does your child feel safe in this school?
- Do the teachers show an interest in your child's learning?
- Do employers find the school's graduates well-prepared for the workforce?
- Do colleges find the school's graduates well-prepared?

If most participants don't return their surveys, then the few surveys that are returned may be from people who are atypical—either unusually satisfied or unusually dissatisfied. Yet these are excellent questions to ask yourself as your child progresses from grade to grade within the school. You can also get some of this information by talking to your child, other students, parents, graduates, and employers on an informal basis.

HOW CAN PUBLISHED SCHOOL INFORMATION MISLEAD US?

Average test scores can mislead if many students are exempt from testing. Students with learning disabilities or limited English proficiency may be exempted from testing. School districts can raise test scores by classifying as many students as possible into these categories or by holding back students until they are able to pass the test. (See "To Test or Not to Test?")

TO TEST OR NOT TO TEST?

Two nearby schools in upstate New York, two groups of students taking standardized tests, two different results. That's what has been happening for years at "Castleton" and "Riverton" Elementary Schools. Castleton students do well on standardized tests, but the school doesn't receive any awards. The school's principal is proud anyway. Everyone, even the "disabled" students, are tested, and some of them pass. "We actually get people out of special education," the principal claims.

Meanwhile, Riverton Elementary has received a national award and favorable press coverage for its students' outstanding performance. Ninety-six percent of Riverton's students pass the state examinations. Yet according to researchers, half of the sixty-eight students in Riverton's K–2 classes had flunked or been placed in special classes. Their scores were excluded from the school averages. If the scores had been included, Riverton's pass rate would have dropped by 18 percentage points.

What's the moral of this story? When schools don't test many of their students, comparisons among schools become misleading. Castleton and Riverton are difficult to compare, because Riverton's test scores provide a distorted picture of its success. Ask the principal of your child's school what percentage of the students were tested in each grade, and remember, the higher, the better.[9]

The tests that are given may be too easy for advanced students, making it impossible for them to demonstrate what they know and hiding whether the students have actually advanced over the course of the year. It means little that a student can pass the third-grade test at the end of the year if she could have passed it at the beginning of the year as well.[10]

Courses may be mislabeled. Courses labeled as "regular" may actually be remedial. "Honors" or "college preparatory" courses may fail to challenge the students or prepare them for college. For instance, "honors" high-school physics in one South Texas school district consisted of elementary school physics with no mathematics required.[11]

Dropout rates can be misleading. Problems with calculated graduation and dropout rates include:

- Students who move away but do not drop out may be mistakenly counted as dropouts.
- Students who drop out may be counted as simply having moved away.
- Students who drop out and then come back only to drop out again are often counted more than once. If a student is counted only once as a dropout but twice as a member of the general student population, then the measured dropout rate is lower than what it should be.
- Ignoring students who drop out during the summer—who simply don't show up to enroll in school in the fall—also lowers the dropout rate. (See "The Dropout Numbers Game.")

THE DROPOUT NUMBERS GAME

Counting students should be a simple thing. Yet when it comes to counting dropouts, the task is anything but easy.

Suppose that a school has ten students enrolled over a full calendar year. Now, suppose that three students leave the school. Two leave during the summer, and one during the school year. Portland, Oregon, calculated its dropout rates by adding the total number of dropouts during the school year and dividing that number by the total enrollment. If our imaginary school was in Portland, then its dropout rate would be one divided by ten, or 10 percent.

However, Seattle, Washington, counted all students that left over the full calendar year, and divides that number by the total enrollment. If our imaginary school was in Seattle, its dropout rate would be three divided by ten, or 30 percent. The method of counting dropouts can make a huge difference![12]

WHAT CAN I DO IF IMPORTANT SCHOOL INFORMATION IS NOT AVAILABLE?

Important school information may be unavailable for one of two reasons:

The school or school district may not produce or collect the information. For example, the district may not give the before-and-after assessments needed for information on students' academic gains.

The school or school district may not make the information available in the form that you need. For example, schools may have information on grades and test scores for each student but never tabulate the information to show how the "A" students as a group did on the test.

Evaluating a school without information on students'
academic gains can be like evaluating the effectiveness
of a new drug based on patients' opinions alone.

If the information is collected but is not tabulated in the form that you need—as in our example of student grades and test scores—the questions to ask are:

Is the information stored in paper records or a computer database? If the information is in a database, it should be easy to retabulate the information in different ways.

Is the information available free of charge? If there is a charge, is it reasonable?

How long does it take the district to supply the information? Some districts have a treasure trove of information but are not set up to respond well to the public's requests for information. Could the district's database be set up to make this process easier and faster?[13]

What can you do if you find out that the information you want is not readily available?

Talk to other parents and get them interested in the problem.

Talk to teachers and school administrators.

Talk to school board members.

Talk to local and state business and school reform leaders.

HOW CAN I GET AN INDEPENDENT PROFESSIONAL EVALUATION OF MY CHILD'S SCHOOL?

Few shareholders of a business would be satisfied without an independent professional audit of the business's financial condition. Parents and taxpayers might similarly benefit from an independent audit of a school's academic quality.

Yet independent professional evaluations of school effectiveness are rare in the United States. Private schools and public school districts do not give high priority to hiring outsiders to take a skeptical look at the schools' effectiveness.

Finding a good independent school evaluator—someone with a strong knowledge of management and education, who could also be impartial—would not be an easy task. Ideally this person or organization would evaluate a number of schools to make it easier to make comparisons. You may want to get together a group of people in your school who are interested in this idea and see if anyone on the local school board (or the private school's board of directors) is interested.[14]

WHAT CHOICES ARE AVAILABLE
IF I NEED TO CHANGE SCHOOLS?

Find out your school district's transfer policy. Some districts make it easy to transfer to another school—all you have to do is ask. This policy is called *open enrollment*. Others have no official policy, but will still give you a transfer if you give them a reason. Contact the school district office to find out which schools are available to you.

You probably have more school choices than you realize:

Other regular public schools may be preferable to your child's current school. Talk to parents who have children there. Ask about academic programs and test scores, and visit the school.

Magnet schools are public schools that have programs that appeal to students with particular interests, such as art, drama, science, career, or technical training. Magnet schools first became widespread in the 1970s as a way to integrate schools by attracting people from different neighborhoods. Find out if there are any local magnet schools, and if so, what the requirements are for admission to those schools.

Charter schools are public schools created to be independent of the school district's central administration. Typically, a group of teachers, parents, or both will apply to the state or the school district for a charter to operate the school independent of most local and state regulations.

Private schools exist in a wide variety of price ranges—some are little more expensive than the day care programs in which many parents enroll their preschool children. For example, the average Catholic elementary school tuition in 1993-94 was less than $250 a month for a nine-month school year. A relatively small minority of private school students are enrolled in the expensive schools that many people associate with the label "private school." Many private schools offer scholarships to students whose parents cannot afford tuition. In addition, privately funded scholarship programs are available in many communities.[16]

CHECKLIST: BEFORE THE SCHOOL VISIT

Information to Request   Received

Published information on   ☐
class sizes, teacher turnover, test
scores, programs, and special
services. Ask if a "school report
card" is available. Get descriptions of programs and courses
offered at the school.

The school's curriculum   ☐
(content standards) for each
grade and subject.

Information on the school's   ☐
performance standards, such
as work samples or descriptions
of the school's standards for excellent, good, and satisfactory
work.

                                                                ☐
Summary of any external
evaluations of the school by
external accrediting agencies.

                                                                ☐
The school's improvement
plan, mission statement, budget,
and discipline policy. Find out if
the school has documented the
implementation and success of
its improvement plans in previous years.

Information to Request	Received
Published school directory, phone numbers of PTA/PTO officers, and campus map. Use the directory to see if anyone you know has children at the school.	☐
Recent Parent-Teacher Association (PTA or PTO) newsletter and minutes. Find out how many members the PTA has and inquire about parent participation on school advisory, planning, and discipline committees.	☐

What to Do	Done
Talk to parents whose children attend the school and ask them about the school's specific strengths and weaknesses.	☐
Arrange to visit classes while they are in progress and meet with the principal.	☐
Write down questions in advance; use the directory to identify who to speak with about each question.	☐

CHECKLIST: DURING THE SCHOOL VISIT

What to Do	Source	Done
Regarding Students:		
Visit as many classrooms as you can.		
Observe student work and classroom discussions. Look at displays of student work in classrooms and hallways.		☐
Ask for samples of **acceptable, good, and excellent student work** if you haven't already received these.	Teacher	☐
Ask for a copy of the **student newspaper and other publications,** such as an anthology of students' creative writing.	School office	☐
Observe student behavior in the lunchroom, outdoor play area, and study hall.		
Regarding School Programs and Staff:		
Find out about **academic, artistic, and athletic extracurricular activities.**	Principal	☐
Discuss **academic, career, and personal counseling.**	Counselor	☐

What to Do	Source	Done
Find out about **tutoring** and other programs for students who fall behind; ask for documentation of these programs' results.	Principal, resource teacher	☐
Find out about availability of **foreign language training.**	Principal	☐
Find out about availability of **Advanced Placement courses and the International Baccalaureate program (high school).**	Principal	☐
Find out about the teachers' training: college degrees in subjects other than education and any specialized training they have received.	Principal	☐

Regarding Facilities and Resources:

Look at **science laboratories, art and music resources, and library and computer facilities.**	Teachers	☐
Note the **overall appearance** of the campus.		☐

CHECKLIST: SCHOOL PRIORITIES AND PLANS

What to Do	Source	Done
Find out how many academic and artistic events (science fairs, art shows, plays, spelling bees, family math nights) the school sponsors.	Principal	☐
Find out how student and parent interest and attendance at these events compares with the attendance at the school's sports events.	Parents, teachers, students	☐
Find out whether most of the school's students think it's "cool" to be successful in school.	Parents, teachers, students	☐
Find out how the prestige of the school's academic stars compares with that of its athletic stars.	Parents, teachers, students	☐
Compare the salaries of experienced teachers with that of the head football coach.	Principal, teachers	☐

Plans:

Get a copy of the school's improvement plan.	Principal	☐

What to Do	Source	Done

Look for:

- Specific, measurable goals ☐
- Goals that have the highest priority ☐
- Ways the goals are measured ☐
- Specific steps designed to reach the goals ☐
- Who is responsible for each step ☐
- Estimates of cost and time required ☐
- Whether previous years' goals were accomplished ☐
- Analysis of why goals were missed in the past ☐

CHECKLIST: ACADEMIC RESULTS

What to Do	Source	Done
Identify reasons to compare schools: to identify the best schools overall or in specific subjects; to identify the best school for your child.		☐
Make "apples-to-apples" comparisons: Look at academic gains; compare how schools do with similarly prepared students; watch out for schools that exempt many students from testing.		☐
Find out what skills the school measures.	Principal, district office	☐

Information to Request	Source	Done
Students' academic gains, by grade level and subject area.	Principal, district office	☐
Average test scores and gains for different groups of students: those who start out ahead, on grade level, or behind; A, B, and C students; students enrolled at least two years.	Principal, district office	☐
Number of students exempted from standardized testing, and the reasons why they were exempted.	Principal, district office	☐

Information to Request	Source	Done
Number of students enrolled in Advanced Placement and other advanced courses; number of students passing Advanced Placement tests (high school).	Principal, district office	☐
Student academic awards and participation in academic competitions.	Principal, district office	☐
Student graduation rates.	Principal, district office	☐
Evidence of success after graduation: how students do in the next higher level of education or in the workforce.	Principal, district office	☐
Results of surveys of parents, teachers, students, and employers.	Principal, district office	☐

CHECKLIST: MAKING INFORMATION AVAILABLE

What to Do	Source	Done
Find out what information is readily available in published reports. Find out if your state or district publishes "school report cards" with information on each campus.	Principal, district office	☐
Look closely to see if the available information is misleading due to course mislabeling, test exemptions, easy tests, and poorly measured dropout and graduation rates.		☐
Find out how long the district takes to supply information that is not in published reports, and how much the district charges for it.	Principal, district office	☐
When information is missing, find out why it is not available:		
• **The information is never produced:** students aren't assessed, or the assessments don't provide the right information.		☐
• **The information isn't entered into a computer database.** Information that must be tabulated laboriously by hand is usually not available.		☐

What to Do	Source	Done
• **The information is in a database but is not available to the public at a reasonable time and cost.**		☐
Work to make important information available. Talk to other parents, teachers, administrators, school board members, and business and community leaders.		☐
Find out about your legal right to information through Open Records legislation in your state.	State education agency	☐
Find out whether others are interested in a professional outside evaluation of the schools' effectiveness.		☐

NOTES

1. The expression "data drought" is taken from Chester Finn, "What to Do about Education: The Schools," *Commentary* (October 1994), referring to the problem that "in most communities one cannot obtain timely, intelligible information about how well one's own children are learning, how their school is doing in relation to other schools, and how the community and state are performing in comparison with the rest of the country and the world."

2. This occurred in the late 1980s. H. G. Bissenger, *Friday Night Lights: A Town, a Team, a Dream* (Reading, Mass.: Addison-Wesley Publishing, 1990), 146.

3. Some schools have few programs because they don't have the money to pay for them. Others have the money but don't spend it well. Schools also differ in their ability to persuade taxpayers and potential contributors that additional money given to them will be well spent. See chapter 11 for ideas on how to get taxpayers to pay for good schools.

4. School evaluation systems that follow these principles are called "value added" systems. The value that is added is intended to represent what the school contributed to the students' knowledge in the course of a year.

Value-added school comparisons require the school district to give similar tests to the same students in successive years. For example, testing students in fourth and fifth grades can make fourth-to-fifth-grade-gains measures available. If students are only tested in fourth and eighth grades, then a measure of fourth-to-eighth-grade gain may be available, but separate measures are not available for each year within that period. This makes it hard to measure the effectiveness of the different schools in which the students were enrolled during that time.

5. Teachers of gifted students must also work unusually hard to keep the students challenged and stay ahead of the class.

6. Mary K. Tallent-Runnels and Ann C. Candler-Lotven, *Academic Competitions for Gifted Students* (Thousand Oaks, Calif.: Corwin Press, 1996), 3–8.

7. This information is called the "longitudinal graduation rate." The word longitudinal means that the district keeps track of the same students over time.

8. Public-school alumni who have little money to contribute often work for employers who do.

9. Bill Zlatos, "Don't Test, Don't Tell," *American School Board Journal* (November 1994): 24-28.

10. This is called the "ceiling effect" problem in testing.

11. Author's conversation with LBJ School work-study student, summer 1994.

12. Glynn Ligon, Bridget Stewart, and David Wilkinson, "Making Dropout Rates Comparable: An Analysis of Definitions and Formulas" (paper presented at the annual meeting of the American Educational Research Association, Boston, Mass., 1990). Austin Independent School District, publication no. 89.22, available from Educational Research Service, 2000 Clarendon Blvd., Arlington, Va., 22201, 703-243-2100.

13. To get answers to questions about the district's assessments, talk to the district's director of student testing. In a small district, the person with this responsibility may be a curriculum director or school principal. The state education agency and a nearby university should also have someone who is knowledgeable about testing. The district's testing director should be able to refer you to the person who knows how the district keeps its data.

14. Schools in the United Kingdom are evaluated every several years by school inspectors who work for the national Ministry of Education. Given the lack of trust of the federal government in the United States, it is difficult to imagine a similar arrangement here. However, nonprofit groups could sponsor such evaluations if parents showed that they were interested.

Some private schools are periodically reviewed by school accreditation organizations. If your child is in private school, you may want to ask when the last accreditation visit occurred and get a copy of the report that came from the visit. What evidence of school effectiveness did the accrediting body examine? Did the visitors look at student performance gains as well as levels? Were any comparisons made with other schools?

15. Only about 13.5 percent of private-school students were enrolled in schools with annual tuitions over $5,000, while 58 percent were in private schools with yearly tuitions of $2,500 or less. Private elementary schools are cheaper than private high schools: average elementary school tuition is $2,138 per year, while high-school tuitions average $4,578. U.S. Department of Education, Digest of Education Statistics: 1995 (Washington, D.C., 1995), 72, table 60.

In the fall of 1996, privately funded scholarship programs existed in twenty-six communities. For up-to-date information on scholarship programs in your community, contact the Center for Education Reform, 1001 Connecticut Avenue, N.W., Suite 204, Washington, D.C., 20036, 800-521-2118. See their Web page (http://edreform.com) under "Selected Reforms at a Glance."

PART TWO

Making Schools Better

5

Preventing Academic Failure

John is entering the third grade and is having difficulty learning how to read.

Mary, a sixth-grader, received an A in mathematics on her last report card but is confused by fractions and percentages.

Shane is so bored with high school that he occasionally skips classes.

QUESTIONS ADDRESSED IN THIS CHAPTER

- What conditions place my child in danger of academic failure?
- What can I do to prevent academic failure?
- How can I make sure my child becomes a good reader?
- What do I do if my child has already fallen behind?
- What do I do if my child has been diagnosed as having a learning disability?
- How can the local schools prevent academic failure?

Your child can fail academically even if he is staying in school and getting good grades. What is academic failure? It's when his schoolwork falls below his age or grade level. If he doesn't get help, he's likely to leave high school poorly prepared for work, college, citizenship, or lifelong learning.

To prevent academic failure, follow the same rules that you would for preventing fires: be aware of hazardous conditions, keep a close watch for the first sign of trouble, and move in quickly and effectively if trouble starts.

Students who cannot read well by the end of third grade are in grave danger of doing poorly for the rest of their years in school.[1]

**WHAT CONDITIONS PLACE MY CHILD
IN DANGER OF ACADEMIC FAILURE?**

He does not master important skills, particularly reading, in early elementary school (grades 1–3). If he can't easily read books about history, science, and other subjects by fourth grade, he will have trouble learning those subjects. He's also headed for trouble if he doesn't learn how to write well or understand basic mathematical concepts.

He has just moved to a new and impersonal school. If he feels that "nobody knows me or cares if I am there," this will hurt his motivation to do well in school.

Large schools can become more personal by dividing teachers into small teams, each of which works with a manageable number of students.

His school has low academic standards and does not expect him to do challenging work. Some middle and high schools allow students to take easy courses in which little learning takes place, and other schools even encourage or assign students to take such courses.[2] Middle and high school should prepare your child to do college-level work even if he does not plan to attend college.

He has many friends who put down academic learning. Especially if he is older, his friends have a powerful influence on what he thinks and does. If his friends put down academic learning, then he may do so too.

He lacks clear rules at home that require him to put learning and schoolwork first. He may pursue many interests, but none of these should be allowed to keep him from being successful in school.

He is not receiving enough attention from adults. Spend as much time with him as your personal circumstances will allow. Find after-school activities that have good adult supervision.

You may want to pay a visit to your child's after-school program to make sure that the children or teenagers are well supervised.

WHAT CAN I DO TO PREVENT ACADEMIC FAILURE?

Make sure your child can read well. Reading is critical for academic success.

Keep track of what he is learning. Contact his teacher(s) regularly about his progress. Find out if your school is successful at teaching important skills to nearly all children. Pay close attention to his learning in the areas in which the school is weak.

Get help quickly if he starts to fall behind. Many schools have special programs and services, but often students don't receive help until they have already fallen far behind. Don't wait until he is far behind to get help!

Find out whether anyone keeps track of how effective are the programs for catching up students who have fallen behind. How many of their students ever catch up? Do teachers and other students have low expectations for the participants in these programs? (Negative labels, such as "slow learner" and "not college material," reveal low expectations.)

Don't lower your standards for your own child. If he falls behind in math, for example, do not assume that he's "just not good in math." Don't let others label him that way, either. He could fall behind for all kinds of reasons: a bad experience in a particular classroom, a teaching method that wasn't well suited for him, lack of a key skill or concept, or lack of enough practice or experience in the subject.

Establish clear rules and priorities in your own home. Make sure that he does his homework every night, and make it easy for him to do so; establish a place for him to study undisturbed, and let him know that his schoolwork is his most important job (see chapter 11).

Spend time talking to him about the importance of school, hard work, and the values of honesty, responsibility, and respect. Show him examples of people who have succeeded because they had all of these traits and people who have failed because they lacked them.

Listen to him. Spend as much time with him as possible: "quantity time" is as important as "quality time."

Keep track of who his friends are, and encourage him to spend time around people who will be a good influence. Notice whether his friends discourage him from studying and doing well in school. Know and talk to their parents. Sign him up for after-school activities that will be a positive influence. Look for academic clubs and artistic programs—not just sports. Inquire about community- or church-sponsored programs as well.

HOW CAN I MAKE SURE MY CHILD BECOMES A GOOD READER?

Read to your child every day. For a preschool child, make sure that he can see the page and that he knows that the story comes from the words, not just the pictures. After he learns how to read, take turns reading to each other. Even after he is an excellent reader and enjoys reading on his own, he will still enjoy having you read to him.

Make sure he has the essential skills for reading, such as knowledge of letter names and sounds and the ability to hear separate sounds in words (for example, the ability to hear three separate sounds in the word *cat*). These are "prereading skills" because children can and should learn them before they can read; for example, most three-year-olds can learn the names and sounds of the letters of the alphabet, but few can read (see chapter 2).

Keep track of his reading level. If he has a third-grade reading level, he can easily read books written for third-graders but will have trouble reading and understanding books written for older children. He will probably score close to the third-grade level on a standardized reading test. See your librarian for a list of popular children's books

Have him read silently at least fifteen minutes every evening once he can read on his own. Keep a daily record of how much your child is reading; post this information on the refrigerator to motivate your child to read more.

Encourage him to write. Writing can focus his attention on spelling, sentence structure, and the value of print as a way of communicating. If he is very young, he must develop the ability to manipulate small objects with his hands before he can hold a pencil and form the letters.

Turn off the television set. The fewer hours the set is on, the more interested he is likely to be in reading. Some families establish such rules as "The television is off after 6 P.M. on weeknights."[3]

Talk to the teacher if you're concerned about your child's reading. Find out what the teacher is doing in the classroom to help him, and have her tell you the things you can do at home to help too. (See "Is Your Child on Track to Be a Good Reader?")

IS YOUR CHILD ON TRACK TO BE A GOOD READER?

To get a good start in reading, your child should:

- Know the names and sounds of all of the letters of the alphabet by the end of kindergarten. Ideally, he would learn these before he enters kindergarten.
- Have sound awareness by the beginning of first grade (age six or so). He should be able to hear three sounds in the word *fish*—note that there are four letters but only three sounds. Good ways to teach sound awareness are nursery rhymes, Dr. Seuss books, identifying words with the same beginning sound (cat, car, cup, and cape) and blending letter sounds to make words ("mmmmaaaaaannnnn" to make *man*).

- Begin reading by the middle of first grade. Good tests of your child's ability to read are his ability to read books he has never seen before and read nonsense words, such as "blug."
- Be able to read chapter books—books with several chapters and many words—by the middle of second grade, or by early third grade at the latest.

Get help for your child if he starts to fall behind. If he is in first or second grade and not yet reading, there is a possibility that he's simply a "late bloomer" who will catch up without help. But the safe choice is to get extra assistance, which can only help him. Some experts recommend tutoring if he hasn't started to read by Thanksgiving of the first-grade year.[4]

Get help immediately if your child is reading
a year or more below grade level.

**WHAT SHOULD I DO IF MY CHILD
HAS ALREADY FALLEN BEHIND?**

Ask your child's teachers to work with you to develop a plan to get him up to speed. The teacher has the responsibility to develop such a plan, explain it to you, and change it as necessary to make it work.

You have the responsibility to help carry out the plan. For example, if he must do thirty minutes a day of math homework to get caught up, your job is to make sure he does so.

Get academic help for him in any skills in which he is weak. One-to-one tutoring is the most powerful and beneficial kind of academic help he can get and is most effective if the tutor is a trained individual who follows an organized curriculum.[5]

Get the school to help you identify ways to get assistance. The school may fail to recognize the existence of a problem if it has not yet become serious. Be persistent—you don't want to wait until the problem becomes serious!

Find out whether the teachers and administrators in the school are using programs that have a track record of success. See if any teachers in the school have had good success in helping students catch up quickly.

> Find out what tutoring programs your school or community has—ask the teacher or school counselor. See the appendix for more information.

Teach your child the skills at home. You can be a one-to-one tutor. Resources to help you do so are listed in the appendix.

If your child's friends are part of the problem, get your child into activities that will help him make new ones. If he is a teenager, his friends are likely to be a greater influence on him than you are. Friends who put down school can hold your child back.

WHAT DO I DO IF MY CHILD HAS BEEN DIAGNOSED AS HAVING A LEARNING DISABILITY?

State and federal laws regulate how education should be provided to students with disabilities.[6] A full discussion of this subject is beyond the scope of this book. However, there are several things you should know:

Most students with learning disabilities can reach high standards with the right kinds of assistance. For example, dyslexic students can learn to read well with the proper training. If your child has a learning disability, he will need extra help, and the school should provide that help and inform you how you can help your child at home.

Some students may be classified by some schools as having learning disabilities when the school cannot figure out how to educate them. This is especially true of students who have not learned how to read.[7]

Find out what percentage of students in the school
are classified as having learning disabilities.
Compare this with the percentages in other public schools.
(Private schools may have lower percentages as a
result of the schools' admissions policies.)

If your child is put in "special education," see if there is evidence of the effectiveness of this program. Does anyone ever get out of special education? How are the academic goals for the students set, and do they usually meet them? Work with the special education teacher to help set *your* child's goals and make sure that he meets them. (See "What Should You Expect from Your Child's Special Education Teacher?")

Find out how your child's academic learning is evaluated. Does he take the same tests as the other students? If not, is his learning assessed regularly? Is his progress compared to the same standards that are applied to students not in special education?

WHAT SHOULD YOU EXPECT FROM YOUR CHILD'S SPECIAL EDUCATION TEACHER?

To help you work effectively with your child, the teacher should:

- Explain your child's learning disability to you in language you can understand. What does your child have difficulty doing and why?
- Design an individual educational plan (IEP) for your child. This plan should follow the rules of good planning discussed in chapter 4: establish specific, measurable goals; identify the steps needed to reach the goals; create a timetable for taking the steps and reaching the goals; measure whether the goals were reached; and identify who is responsible for making sure all of this happens.
- Carry out the plan. Plans do little good if they are ignored. See chapter 10 on accountability for what to do if there is a problem with this.

- Tell you what you can do to help your child learn. "Your responsibility is to do these things ..."
- Keep you informed about his progress. If he isn't progressing as he should, you need to know as early as possible.
- Make needed changes in instruction if he isn't learning.

Just because your child has been diagnosed with a learning disability is no reason for you or the school to abandon high academic standards. Many individuals with learning disabilities have been very successful in college and in life.[8]

HOW CAN THE LOCAL SCHOOLS PREVENT ACADEMIC FAILURE?

You have a large stake in how good your local schools are at preventing academic failure. If the students are better prepared, this increases the odds that your child will do well. Failing students are more likely to get involved in crime and gangs.[9]

Here's a short list of what schools and school districts can do:

Give priority to preventing failure in the early grades, rather than treating it once it has gotten out of hand. If children are falling off a cliff, it's better to build a fence at the top of the cliff than to station an ambulance at the bottom.[10]

Reduce the hazardous conditions that produce academic failure. Educators can't control all of the problems in homes and neighborhoods that place students at risk. However, they can do several things:

- Do a good job of teaching the basics of reading, writing, and mathematics in elementary school.
- Operate middle and high schools that give personal attention to each individual student. Chronically absent or late students should receive telephone calls or home visits telling them how much the teachers want them to come to school.
- Educate parents about ways they can help their children succeed in school.

- Make parents feel welcome in the school building, and listen to their ideas.
- Organize parent groups that can have a good influence on other parents. Parents will often listen to other parents. One elementary school in a low-income housing project in Dallas, Texas, recruited parents as block volunteers to make sure their fellow parents got their children to school on time.
- Work with parents and local agencies to see that students' physical and health-care needs are taken care of. A child with a toothache has a hard time concentrating on his studies.

Identify which programs produce the best results per dollar spent, and look for ways to reallocate money from less to more effective programs. How much good does $1,000 invested in Program A do, compared with Program B?

Identify how many students need academic help in each grade level. The school or school district should also identify the subject(s) in which the students need help.

Estimate the cost of giving adequate help to every student who needs it. This cost should be broken out by grade level. For example, your district may be able to tutor every student who needs it at relatively low cost.[11]

Make a pitch to taxpayers and community leaders when funds are short. People in many communities have a strong desire to help schools if they believe that the money will be well spent.

CHECKLIST: PREVENTING ACADEMIC FAILURE

What You Need to Do	Source	Done
Make sure your child can read at or above grade level and get help quickly if he starts to fall behind.	Teacher, tutoring program	☐
Regularly contact his teacher to discuss what he's learning.	Teacher	☐
Find out how his learning is assessed.	Teacher, chapter 3	☐
Beware of schools or courses with low standards.		☐
Know your child's friends and their parents. Encourage him to keep friends who enjoy school and learning.		☐
Make school attendance and homework his first priority.		☐
Spend as much time with him as possible.		☐
Find good after-school supervision for him.	School counselor, churches, community organizations	☐
Have high standards for him in all of his subjects.		☐

What You Need to Do	Source	Done
Find out how many students catch up who receive remedial instruction or other special academic services.	Principal	☐
Do not lower your standards even if your child has learning disabilities.		☐
Find out how many children in special education return to regular classrooms and do grade-level work.	Principal	☐

NOTES

1. See Lloyd, "Prediction of School Failure"; and Kraus, *Yesterday's Children.*

2. Offering high-standards courses to some students and low-standards courses to others is called curricular tracking, as discussed in chapter 6.

3. See Aletha C. Huston, Edward Donnerstein, Halford Fairchild, Norma D. Feshbach, Phyllis A. Katz, John P. Murray, Eli A. Rubinstein, Brian L. Wilcox, and Diana Zuckerman, eds., *Big World, Small Screen* (University of Nebraska Press, 1992).

4. Two of these experts are Philip Gough, Department of Psychology, University of Texas at Austin, and George Farkas, developer of the Reading One-One tutoring program, University of Texas at Dallas. The Reading Recovery program also emphasizes the importance of tutoring students in first grade.

5. George Farkas, "Structured Tutoring for At-Risk Children in the Early Years," *Applied Behavioral Science Review* 555: 127–142; Barbara A. Wasik and Robert E. Slavin, "Preventing Early Reading Failure with One-to-One Tutoring: A Review of Five Programs," *Reading Research Quarterly* 28-2: 178–200.

6. The most important federal legislation is the Individuals with Disabilities Education Act (20 United States Code, 1400–85), which requires school districts to provide "free appropriate public education" to all disabled students between the ages of three and twenty-two who are residents of the district.

7. How this can happen is explained in Louise Spear-Swerling and Robert J. Sternberg, *Off Track: When Poor Readers Become "Learning Disabled"* (New York: Westview Press, 1996). See also Robert Slavin, Nancy Karweit, and Barbara Wasik, *Preventing Early School Failure* (Needham Heights, Mass.: Allyn and Bacon, 1994).

8. See Carol Tingey and Lance Mortensen, *A Longitudinal Follow-up Study of 284 Adults Classified As Learning Disabled When They Were Second Graders: Final Report* (Logan: Utah State University). Available as ED document number 385108 through the ERIC Document Reproduction Service, 7420 Fullerton Road, Suite 110, Springfield, Va., 22153-2852, 800-443-3742, edes@inet.ed.gov. The corresponding Web page is at http://www.edrs.com.

9. The technical phrase for "fellow-student effects" is "contextual effects." See Stephen W. Raudenbush and J. Douglas Willms, "The Estimation of School Effects," *Journal of Educational and Behavioral Statistics* 20, no. 4 (Winter 1995): 307–35.

One study found that effective educational intervention in *preschool* reduces crime rates when the children grow up. See Steven Barnett and Colette Escobar, "Research on the Cost Effectiveness of Early Educational Intervention: Implications for Research and Policy," *American Journal of Community Psychology* (December 1989): 677-704.

10. This metaphor is taken from Slavin, Karweit, and Wasik, *Preventing Early School Failure*, ix-x.

11. George Farkas, Jim Fischer, Keven Vicknair, and Ralph Dosher, "Can *All* Students Learn to Read at Grade-Level by the End of Third Grade?" (Dallas: Center for Education and Social Policy, University of Texas at Dallas, 1995).

6

Raising Academic Standards

If we expect kids to be losers they will be losers; if we expect them to be winners they will be winners. They rise, or fall, to the level of the expectations of those around them, especially their parents and teachers.
— *Jaime Escalante, award-winning California mathematics teacher*

QUESTIONS ADDRESSED IN THIS CHAPTER

- Why do some schools have low standards?
- What do we know about high academic standards?
- How can I help my child reach high academic standards?
- How can my child's school challenge gifted students?
- What can I do to help raise standards in my child's school or school district?

Every student deserves an academically challenging education. Chances are, you know of students whose minds are not adequately challenged. There are two basic approaches to raising standards:

Increase the standard for acceptable work. For example, teachers can raise the standard for passing work in their classes, and school districts can increase the requirements for high-school graduation.

Increase the number of students whose work meets advanced standards—standards of excellence far above the minimum. For example, the school can increase the number of students who qualify for advanced placement in college or who complete difficult and challenging research projects.

When schools are full of poorly prepared students,
this may be used as an argument against raising standards.
Instead, it's a reason to put in better programs to prevent
cademic failure while we raise standards (see chapter 5).

WHY DO SOME SCHOOLS HAVE LOW STANDARDS?

Parents and the public may expect too little. Parents may be happy if their children learn "what I learned in school," but if schools were mediocre in the past, that's not enough. Schools in many high-poverty neighborhoods have a history of low achievement, so parents may believe this is normal.

Many students and parents treat education as a process for "getting papers that certify they are competent, rather than developing real competence," to use Andrei Toom's apt words.[1] Why work hard for a grade or a diploma if the school can make it easy? Employers support this view by paying attention only to the diploma, not to how much the student learned.

Teachers have little time to work together toward the goal of raising standards. It's easier for each teacher to impose higher requirements on students if all teachers do, so that students can't use the example of Mr. So-and-So down the hall whose students don't have to work so hard.

School districts lack programs and plans to implement high standards and help students reach them. Without a workable plan, a school district may have trouble convincing taxpayers to fund the required programs. Many school districts have no coherent plans at all; their goals are vague and they have no idea of how to reach the goals. (See chapter 4 on the elements of a workable plan and chapter 11 on school district planning.)

Some educators and parents believe that average or academically delayed students can't reach high standards. As a result, many schools provide a first-rate education for only a few students, while enrolling others in courses where the students don't learn much. This practice, called curricular tracking, has given many students in the United States an inadequate education.2 (See "What Is Curricular Tracking?")

> Make sure your child is enrolled in courses that challenge her and educate her to high standards. For information on how to identify these courses, talk to teachers and counselors and read chapters 1 and 2.

WHAT IS CURRICULAR TRACKING?

Does your child's high school have college preparatory, general, and vocational tracks? Does your middle school have honors and regular courses? (These courses and tracks may have different names.) If some of these courses have low academic standards, then your school has curricular tracking—the practice of offering challenging courses to some students and easy, unchallenging courses to others.

Curricular tracking is different from three legitimate practices:

- **True remediation.** The purpose of a true remedial program is to get students who are behind to catch up as quickly as possible. Thus, the program expects those students to study harder and learn *faster*. For this reason, true remediation is sometimes called *acceleration*. Tracked courses, on the other hand, give *less* work to the students who are behind and give them work that is so easy that they never catch up.
- **Prerequisite courses.** Students should master Algebra I before taking Algebra II.
- **Different courses for students with different interests.** Some students may be interested in the arts, others in math and science, and still others in preparing early for careers. The questions to ask are: Do these programs prepare the students to do college-level work, whether or not they intend to go to college? Do all of the students receive a strong background in academic subjects outside their areas of specialization?

WHAT DO WE KNOW ABOUT HIGH ACADEMIC STANDARDS?

When standards are raised, students, teachers, and parents rise to the challenge. Between 1984 and 1990, forty-two states toughened their high-school graduation requirements, and yet graduation rates showed little decline. In addition, a higher percentage of U.S. high-school students are taking advanced courses.[3]

Encouraging students to take advanced courses even helps students who don't take them, when schools upgrade their entire curriculum to prepare students for the courses.

Students from low-income and minority groups do better when standards are raised. Examples of this are:

- Student achievement improved dramatically in a historically low performing Baltimore elementary school that adopted a high-quality private school curriculum.[4]
- A Macy Foundation program that encouraged minority students to take advanced courses was able to get 90 percent of its 2,500 participants to enroll in four-year colleges, from schools that traditionally sent few students to college.[5]
- When Georgia Tech toughened up the standards in its five-week Challenge Program course to prepare entering minority students to succeed, the performance gap between minority and white students disappeared. The program "made it cool (for minority students) to be smart," according to one senior.[6]
- When academic standards were raised in New York City, more than 6,500 additional black students and 7,000 additional Latino students passed challenging science courses.[7]

It's important for elementary and middle schools to prepare students to meet high standards in high school. Several schools in the Macy Foundation program only accepted students who were reading at or above grade level, believing that students needed good reading skills in order to succeed in the program. When standards were raised in New York City, 42 percent of ninth-graders taking advanced courses failed to meet the new, higher standard in mathematics, and 27 percent failed in science.[8]

Find out if your child's elementary or middle school prepares
students well. Do the school's former students excel on
Advanced Placement tests in high school? Do they do well in
academic competitions? Do they do well in college? If your
school district doesn't keep track of this information, talk
to high-school teachers about whether your school
is sending them well-prepared students (see chapter 1).

HOW CAN I HELP MY CHILD
REACH HIGH ACADEMIC STANDARDS?

There are two approaches, which may be named after the hare and
the tortoise in the famous Aesop's fable. The Tortoise Principle is "slow
and steady wins the race"—with the emphasis on "steady." The Hare
Principle might be "fast but inconsistent loses the race."

Students who follow the Hare Principle learn in intense spurts, in-
terrupted by long periods in which little learning takes place. Students who take it easy for a semester and then cram for the final exam
are learning like hares. Often they forget the material almost as
quickly as they learned it.

If you want to follow the Tortoise Principle to get your child to high
standards, here's how:

Make sure there are no wasted years or semesters at school.
If your child has an ineffective teacher, get a good set of books on the
material she's studying from the library and make sure she studies
those books—or get her into a different teacher's class. If the problem
goes beyond one teacher, look at your options for changing schools
(see chapter 4).

Encourage your child to read extra books
on the subject she's studying in any case.

Add a little more learning to each day. Ask "why" questions in the car. Have her read fifteen more minutes a day rather than watching television. Have her study a foreign language fifteen minutes a night. Take her to a bookstore, library, or museum on Saturdays. If she's in elementary school, you may want to form a neighborhood math club whose members eat pizza and learn math together.

Encourage your middle- or high-school student to form a study group with her friends, as many college students do. If her friends aren't interested in studying, help her form a group with other students who are. She may make a better set of friends as a result.

Make sure she keeps learning when school is not in session. Encourage her to read during the summer. Sign her up for an art class or nature course. If you can't afford such a class, ask your employer or another local business to donate a scholarship for your child.

> To reach high standards, increase the amount of
> time your child spends learning—and increase
> the variety of her learning experiences.

When is the Hare Principle appropriate? If your child has fallen behind in school, she may need to run like a hare to catch up. Jaime Escalante was able to get poorly prepared inner-city students to pass the Advanced Placement calculus exam by getting them to run like hares—they came to school early, stayed late, and attended classes on Saturdays.

HOW CAN MY CHILD'S SCHOOL CHALLENGE GIFTED STUDENTS?

Here's what your school can do:

Encourage advanced students to move ahead at their own pace once they've mastered the material that the other students are learning. All students should be encouraged to move ahead whenever they can. Your child may find herself way ahead in one subject, even as she just keeps up with the rest of the class in other subjects.

Encourage advanced students to study the subject in greater depth. If the class is studying the Civil War, advanced students might do a detailed study of the strategies used in particular battles, politics in the North and the South, or the role of freed slaves in the war.

Encourage advanced students to work together on projects. Whatever the school's policy on grouping students, advanced students should have opportunities to work together.

Make advanced classes available for students who have mastered the prerequisites for those classes. This is different from tracking, in that *all* students are encouraged to master the prerequisites and take the classes. To keep standards high, students should be expected to meet a difficult set of requirements in order to pass the course.

Encourage advanced middle- and high-school students to take classes in local colleges and universities. Minnesota has done so since 1985.[9] Over 25,000 students have taken advantage of a similar opportunity in Florida.

WHAT CAN I DO TO HELP RAISE STANDARDS IN MY CHILD'S SCHOOL OR SCHOOL DISTRICT?

Get information about what high standards look like. See chapter 2.

Insist on high academic standards for your own child.

Get a group of parents and teachers together to discuss higher standards. For example, if the school goal is to get more students to pass Advanced Placement exams, you might want to pass around some old exams so that parents can see the kind of work the students will be expected to do.

Support teachers who "take the heat" for raising standards in their classrooms. Some parents may complain when teachers expect students to work harder, so you should let the teacher know you are behind him all the way. (See "How a Teacher Was Fired for Having High Standards.")

Identify schools where large numbers of students meet high standards. This establishes that the standards are attainable.

HOW A TEACHER WAS FIRED FOR HAVING HIGH STANDARDS

Meet Adele Jones, a Georgetown, Delaware, algebra teacher who was fired in 1993 for failing students in her class who didn't learn algebra. "When students go to college with a credit for Algebra II, the college expects them to have learned these concepts," she said. Holding to this standard, in 1991–92 Jones gave Fs to 27 percent of her students and Ds to 26 percent. Her principal argued that low grades would discourage students from taking more math courses and that they were getting better grades from other teachers in the school.

Students protested. "I Failed Ms. Jones' Class and It Was My Fault" read one sign, while others commented that they appreciated getting an A that really meant something. Eventually, Jones was rehired.

Jones was singled out because her grading policies were different from those of other teachers in the school. This case shows that it's hard for one teacher to raise standards unless others do.[10]

If the goal is to raise standards districtwide, talk to community leaders about your goals and get their support. See chapter 11.

Be prepared to answer the objections of parents who oppose high standards:

- "Kids need to relax and enjoy their childhood." Yes, and they need to be prepared to have an interesting adulthood.
- "My child is bored with school." And she may be bored because she isn't being challenged.
- "I want my child to be well-rounded." Well-roundedness includes a first-rate education.
- "My child needs As in order to get into a good college." And she needs to be prepared to do the work once there.
- "My high-schooler is too busy working to help pay the bills." A high-quality education will help your high-schooler pay the bills for the rest of her life.
- "Many of these advanced courses won't help students get a job."

The students who have the most trouble getting jobs are the poorly educated, not the well educated.

- "All students aren't cut out for a traditional academic program." All students aren't cut out for a program that uses traditional *methods*, but nearly all students can master the required *content*.
- "The less-prepared students will just get discouraged and drop out." Let's put in better programs to prevent academic failure, rather than dumbing down the curriculum because we lack those programs.
- "Higher standards won't solve the kids' problems." High standards are an important part of solving *one* problem: the lack of a good education.

CHECKLIST: RAISING ACADEMIC STANDARDS

What You Need to Do	Source	Done
Make sure your child has no wasted semesters or years in school.	Teacher, counselor	☐
Add a little more learning to each day.		☐
Help your child form a study group.		☐
Enroll your child in challenging courses.	Counselor	☐
Make sure your school encourages all students who master prerequisite courses to enroll in advanced courses.	Counselor, principal	☐
Support programs for gifted/ advanced students to learn at their own pace, explore topics in depth, and work together.	Teachers, other parents	☐
Support programs that challenge all students to learn rapidly, explore topics in depth, and work together.	Teachers, other parents	☐
Support effective teachers who have high standards and tough grading practices.	Other parents	☐

What You Need to Do	Source	Done
Get information on high standards; discuss this information with parents and teachers.	Chapter 2, appendix	☐
Identify schools with many students attaining high standards, and share this information	Other parents, community leaders	☐
Be prepared to respond to objections to high standards from other parents.		☐

NOTES

1. Toom, "A Russian Teacher in America."

2. Evidence that many Americans have received a low-quality education comes from the National Assessment of Educational Progress and numerous surveys of the knowledge of students and adults. See chapter 2, note 1.

3. The percentage of students taking calculus increased from 4.3 to 10.1 percent between 1982 and 1992, while the percentage of students taking all of biology, chemistry, and physics rose from 9.8 to 21.6 percent. U.S. Department of Education, National Center for Education Statistics, *The Condition of Education 1994* (Washington, D.C., 1994), 74.

4. Michael Janofsky, "Private School Curriculum Brings Public School Improvement," *New York Times*, February 22, 1995.

5. E. Belvin Williams and Bella August, "Learning from Success: Strategies and Implications," in Robert Berne and Lawrence O. Picus, eds., *Outcome Equity in Education* (Thousand Oaks, Calif.: Corwin Press, 1994), 87–105.

6. Ronald Smothers, "To Raise the Performance of Minorities, a College Increased Its Standards," *New York Times*, June 29, 1994.

7. Karen Diegmueller, "Tougher N.Y.C. Requirements Seen Spurring Gains," *Education Week* (May 17, 1995): 8.

8. For more on the Macy Foundation program, see Williams and August, "Learning from Success," 91.

For a discussion of the New York City standards, see Diegmueller, "Tougher N.Y.C. Requirements"; and Maria Newman, "Shaky 9th Grade Test Result As Math and Science Toughen," *New York Times*, August 31, 1995. At the same time, enrollment in advanced mathematics courses rose from 36,500 to 50,500, so that, even though the pass rate declined, the number of students passing actually rose.

9. Approximately 6 percent of Minnesota high-school juniors and seniors took college courses during the 1994–95 school year. *Postsecondary Enrollment Options Program: March 1996* (St. Paul: Program Evaluation Division, Office of the Legislative Auditor, State of Minnesota, 1996), 11.

10. Ann Bradley, "The High Price of Failure," *Teacher Magazine* (October 1993): 35–39. The article provides evidence that the teacher was conscientious and effective, requiring the students to do their homework and learn the material. The principal believed giving students bad grades was bad policy, whether or not the students had learned the material, because he felt the students would be discouraged from continuing in math.

7

Improving School Safety and Discipline

We become just by the practice of just actions, self-controlled by exercising self-control, and courageous by performing acts of courage.

— *Aristotle*

QUESTIONS ADDRESSED IN THIS CHAPTER

- Is my school safe? Does my school hear the SOS (safety, order, and standards) call of the American public?
- What can improve safety and discipline at school?
- How can I help make my child's school safer?
- What are some ways to make sure my child is well behaved at school?
- What should I do if my child gets in trouble at school?

Parents consistently rank school safety and discipline among their most important concerns. Yet many do not recognize that they, not the schools, have the primary responsibility for raising their children. Astoundingly, 63 percent of U.S. adults think that home and school have equal responsibility for children's personal and social development.[1] High standards of safety and discipline in school begin at home.

The "broken window" theory of crime explains why high disciplinary standards in schools are important. A single unrepaired window shows troublemakers that no one cares, so other windows in the neighborhood get broken. Soon the neighborhood becomes a magnet for people who break windows and commit other crimes.

Likewise, if students see other students getting away with some things, they will test the limits of what they can get away with. If enough do the wrong thing, soon the pressure is on the well-behaved students to join in.

Some parents support discipline in schools all the way — until it comes to their children's behavior. Then they decide that the rules should be bent or that *their* own children couldn't possibly be at fault. Don't be one of those parents!

IS MY SCHOOL SAFE? DOES MY SCHOOL HEAR THE SOS (SAFETY, ORDER, AND STANDARDS) CALL OF THE AMERICAN PUBLIC?

Few adults would tolerate working somewhere where they are afraid to go to work or worried about being bullied when they visit the bathroom. Yet many students tolerate these conditions every day.

The first source of information about school safety is your child. Ask him if he feels safe in school and on the school bus. Of course, the fact that he may feel insecure or threatened does not always mean that he will be injured or bullied on campus. However, if he doesn't feel safe, something is wrong and you need to find out what it is. Is he afraid of particular students? Are some students behaving in ways that repeatedly violate the school rules, and if so, what is being done about it?

Other sources of information on school safety and discipline include:

The school's discipline policy. Usually schools send home a discipline plan at the beginning of the school year. The plan should describe the rules and the consequences of violating those rules. Does the school follow its own plan?

The school's rate of teacher turnover—what percent of the teachers leave every year? Teachers quickly get fed up with schools that have lax standards of safety and discipline. (Of course, high teacher turnover may occur for other reasons as well.)

Informal conversations with other parents, teachers, and students.

Surveys of students and teachers.

Publicly available reports of the number of assaults and other incidents occurring on the campus. This information is likely to be of poor quality, as some incidents may go unreported—possibly because students and teachers are afraid to report them or because administrators do not want to give the school a bad name.

Find out what kinds of school safety–related information you are legally entitled to. For example, in Texas parents and the public are entitled to information on the number of students at a school who are on probation or parole.

WHAT CAN IMPROVE SAFETY AND DISCIPLINE AT SCHOOL?

A clear code of conduct, which is known to everybody and consistently enforced, can make it plain to students what is expected of them.

A no-nonsense principal is an important person in maintaining school safety and discipline. She should help the teachers enforce the school rules consistently. Let her know you will support her efforts to maintain high standards of safety and discipline.

School discipline committees with parent and student participation can help make and enforce the school rules. Parent participation on these committees is particularly important in neighborhoods where parents might otherwise mistrust the school. Student participation can be effective when students are less lenient on their fellow students than the adults would be.[2]

Character education teaches values, such as honesty, respect, and responsibility—the same values you teach at home. Although your child may already practice these, it is surely in his interest that his classmates practice them as well. The teaching may take place through stories told in the classroom, through activities designed to study the "value of the month," or through public recognition of students whose behavior exemplifies good values. For example, a student might receive a bravery award for defending another student who was being attacked by bullies.[3]

Character education was an important part of American schooling for generations. The stories in the McGuffey's Readers, the most popular reading textbooks of the nineteenth century, had such titles as *The Honest Boy and the Thief.* These titles seem quaint to generations that learned many of their values from television.

One-on-one tutoring and mentoring gets students to spend time around adults who are good influences.

Alternative programs remove from the regular classroom students who repeatedly disrupt the class. This enables the teacher and the other students to get on with the business of learning, while giving troubled students the special assistance they need.

Alternative classrooms and in-school suspension keep disruptive students in the school. In some cases, it may be necessary to send the student to a special program at a different campus. To be effective, these programs should teach values, academic skills, and social skills—not just warehouse the students. If your child is disciplined in this way, make sure that he continues to be taught by caring adults—and work with him in the home to make sure the problem doesn't happen again.

> Pay close attention to the effectiveness of these
> alternative programs. Are they good at working
> with the parents as well as the students?

HOW CAN I HELP MAKE MY CHILD'S SCHOOL SAFER?

Parents can help improve or maintain school safety in some critical ways:

Make sure your own child is well behaved. See question 4.

Contact the teacher or principal if your child says he's being bullied, and ask them to make sure the behavior stops. Your child may not tell you he's being bullied, but you should suspect it if he suddenly finds excuses not to ride the bus or go to school. Do not let his fear of retaliation allow bullies to continue their behavior.

Wait with him at the bus stop. All it takes is one parent to keep potentially disruptive children from misbehaving.

Volunteer to ride on the school bus. Safe behavior is even more imperative on a moving bus where children are likely to fall with sudden stops. Loud or active children could make it difficult for the driver to concentrate.

Visit the school yard during the mornings or during scheduled free play periods. Encourage other parents to visit too. Parents can help ensure that all children are safe during those times when they are less supervised.

> Check at the school office to find out what
> rules or guidelines apply for visitors.

Volunteer to be a lunchroom or teacher aide. Lunchrooms tend to group large numbers of students together where it can be difficult to maintain order. Parents can also help teachers in the classroom, freeing the teacher from nonteaching tasks and providing extra help for individual students.

> Volunteering works well. Check into volunteer training
> programs to make the best use of your time.

Report serious misconduct immediately, even if it does not involve your own child. If you feel comfortable doing so, ask the student(s) to stop their behavior immediately and get their names.

Volunteer to assist at school events, such as dances and athletic games. This is especially important for middle- and high-school children because these events tend to be difficult for school staff to monitor alone.

Make sure your school has a visitor policy that requires parents and other visitors to sign in and out when they visit. You may want to suggest parent or visitor badges for any adult who needs to walk throughout the building.

Make sure your school has a child-release policy that allows your child to go home only with the adults that you authorize. This is especially important for young children.

Make sure your school has a policy that the campus be kept clean. This emphasizes the importance of well-kept facilities and teaches children respect for their school and environment.

Ask your school to report school safety and discipline violations to parents and the community. Parents have a right to know how well the school is maintaining safety and discipline. Work with other parents or the PTA to develop a safety report card if one does not exist. (Names of individual students will need to be omitted for privacy reasons.)

WHAT ARE SOME WAYS TO MAKE SURE MY CHILD IS WELL BEHAVED AT SCHOOL?

Learn the school's rules of discipline and the consequences of violating them. Make sure your child learns them, too, and understands the reasons for each rule. Let him know that you know and respect those rules. Get a copy of the school's discipline policy at the beginning of each school year.

Support the school's right to discipline your child at school, even though teachers will sometimes make mistakes. He needs to know that bad behavior at school will get him in trouble twice—once at school and again at home.

Remember that he is likely to behave differently at school than at home. At home, he doesn't spend the day with twenty or thirty other students his age. He may act worse at school because of the influence of his peers—or he may act better because he is around people whose friendship he has to earn.

Visit your child's classroom and observe what goes on there. To get a better picture, visit more than once or volunteer to help out in the room for a day or two. Find out your school's and teacher's policy on class visits, and be sure to enter as quietly as possible during class hours so as not to interrupt the students' work.

Talk to the teacher often—not just at scheduled teacher conferences. Listen to the teacher—her intent is to help your child. Work with the teacher if there is a problem (see chapter 1).

If the teacher calls or sends home notes about your child's behavior, take the problem seriously. Writing notes and calling is burdensome and time consuming for the teacher; doing so tells you that the problem has become serious.

For serious offenses, find out what rule your child broke, and get a copy of any written disciplinary records. Use this information when you discuss the incident with him, so he knows you understand why he is being disciplined.

Give your child consistent rules and consequences at home. The rules should be enforced, and he should understand the reasons for the rules. (See "Three Basic Parenting Styles.")

THREE BASIC PARENTING STYLES

Psychologists have found that there are three basic parenting styles.

Permissive parents see themselves as *caregivers* whose main responsibility is to make their children happy. Permissive parents don't enforce consistent rules because they're afraid of losing their children's love or because they believe that adults don't have the right to tell children what to do. Some permissive parents lack clear ideas of good behavior and are likely to see their children's misbehavior as "cute."

Authoritarian parents see themselves as *bosses* whose main responsibility is to make their children obey. The trouble with this parenting style is that children can get mistaken ideas about right and wrong, such as:

- "The deed is wrong because it causes you to get in trouble" but not so bad if you can get away with it.
- "The deed is wrong because I said so"; as soon as a respected person—such as a gang leader—says that the deed is okay, then it must be okay.

Authoritative parents see themselves as *teachers* whose main responsibility is to teach their children how to be successful, responsible adults. The authoritative parent knows she must also be caregiver and boss. However, the reason why the parent is boss is so that the child can learn from her.

Teach your child good values at home. Discuss and tell stories to illustrate these values. Be aware of the examples you set for your own children.

Spend time talking and listening to him. This enables you to be his teacher.

Counselors can be an invaluable source. Use them!

WHAT SHOULD I DO IF MY CHILD GETS IN TROUBLE AT SCHOOL?

- Listen to the teacher and understand her point of view.
- Make sure your child understands why he got in trouble.
- Work with your child, the teacher, and the school counselor to make sure the problem does not happen again.

CHECKLIST: IMPROVING SCHOOL SAFETY AND DISCIPLINE

What You Need to Do	Source	Done
Ask your child if he feels safe on the bus, school yard, and in school.	Your child	☐
Get a copy of the school discipline policy at the beginning of the year and discuss it with your child.	Teacher, principal	☐
Find out if the school's discipline policy is consistently followed.	Principal, teachers, parents, students	☐
Tell the principal you support high safety and discipline standards and understand it's her job to maintain them.		☐
Find out what the teacher turnover and attendance have been for the past three years.	Principal, district	☐
Find out how the school reports information about safety and discipline (survey results, major rule violations, violent incidents, etc.).	Principal	☐
Find out if the school has a school discipline committee and how parents can be involved.	Principal	☐

What You Need to Do	Source	Done
Find out what programs the school has in place to reinforce high safety and discipline standards.	Principal	☐
Learn at least three ways you can help ensure that your child's school is safe. Choose one or two and do them regularly.		☐
Support the school's right to discipline your child.		☐
Learn how you can help ensure your child is well behaved at school.		☐
Learn the three basic parenting styles.		☐
Work with the teacher or school counselor to develop a plan to monitor and improve your child's behavior if he gets into trouble.	Teacher, counselor, your child	☐

NOTES

1. Center for Educational Research and Innovation, Organization for Economic Cooperation and Development, *Education at a Glance: OECD Indicators* (Washington, D.C.: OECD Publications, 1995), 57, table C24.

2. James Comer, "Educating Poor and Minority Children," *Scientific American* (November 1988): 44–48; and James Comer, *School Power* (New York: Free Press, 1980). In some cases, student privacy laws may limit parent and student participation on these committees. The principal will know if this is the case in your state. Parents can be involved in making rules even when their enforcement must be left to the principal.

3. Typically the values chosen are ones on which there is wide agreement and which are believed to be important for making the school or community a livable place. See Thomas Lickona, *Educating for Character: How Our Schools Can Teach Respect and Responsibility* (New York: Bantam Books, 1992).

8

Improving Classroom Teaching and School Management

A good teacher touches hundreds of lives.

QUESTIONS ADDRESSED IN THIS CHAPTER

- What should I expect from my child's teacher?
- What should I expect from my child's principal?
- What should I do if I have a problem with my child's teacher or principal?
- How can my school or school district improve teachers' effectiveness?

Effective schools have clear goals for student learning, skilled and enthusiastic teachers, and the leadership of an effective principal. You can support your school's and school district's efforts to improve all of these. (See chapter 11 for ways to get involved.)

WHAT SHOULD I EXPECT FROM MY CHILD'S TEACHER?

A good teacher encourages your child to learn. He

Shows knowledge and enthusiasm for the subject he teaches. He knows the subject well, is excited about teaching it, and encourages your child's interest and enthusiasm for learning.

> The teacher will be much more effective if you
> encourage your child's love of learning at home.

173

Challenges your child academically and holds high expectations for her ability to learn. He helps her understand what she needs to learn, encourages her to work hard in order to succeed, and gives her clear feedback on her academic progress.

Encourages her to work thoughtfully and diligently. He encourages her to plan her work, think carefully about what she's doing, and finish projects on time.

A good teacher organizes the learning process. He

Maintains a classroom in which everyone is treated with courtesy and respect.

Organizes the classroom to make effective use of your child's time. When you visit the room, your child and the other students know what they are supposed to do and are actively involved in learning. When students become distracted, the teacher takes steps to bring them back on track.

Finds out what your child knows, and teaches her what she does not know. He assesses your child often enough to be aware of what she already knows. When difficulties arise during the school year, he develops a plan to help her progress.

Communicates clearly about what she has learned and where improvement is needed. You should ask for and receive clear information about what she is supposed to learn and about her success in learning these things.

Helps you get assistance for her if she needs it. If she needs additional help, the teacher is able to direct you to others, such as the school counselor, who can assist in her academic and emotional development.

WHAT SHOULD I EXPECT FROM MY CHILD'S PRINCIPAL?

A good principal supports good classroom teaching. He

Recruits and retains good teachers. The school is a place where good teachers want to teach.

In some school districts, principals have little say
in recruiting teachers to work at the school.
Find out how much say your school's principal has.

Schedules time for teachers to work together and share ideas. He encourages teachers to share their best ideas and experiences with each other.

Observes classrooms and provides feedback to teachers on how they can improve. He may also schedule time for teachers to observe each others' classrooms and provide feedback. This can be especially helpful for new teachers.

Helps teachers get ongoing training to improve their skills. He helps teachers identify what will best meet their needs.

Helps teachers with student discipline problems. He makes sure that the school's rules are fairly and consistently enforced.

Does a good job of matching teachers and students. He oversees assigning students with special needs, gifted students, and those with behavior difficulties to teachers who have the expertise to meet their needs.

Takes appropriate steps when a teacher's students aren't learning. He evaluates carefully whether the teacher should receive professional development, be assigned to a different group of students, or be counseled to seek employment elsewhere. (See "Under What Circumstances Can Teachers Be Let Go?")

UNDER WHAT CIRCUMSTANCES CAN TEACHERS BE LET GO?

In private schools, the school director or principal usually has the power to hire and fire teachers at will. Under this system, parents and school trustees rely on his judgment to make good decisions.

In public schools the principal must document the teacher's poor performance. Letters from parents can be an important part of this documentation. The teacher is put on an improvement plan, and if he fails to improve over the course of a year, the principal can recommend that his contract not be renewed. The teacher can then appeal the principal's decision, following rules established by the state, the local school district, and the teachers' union contract if one exists.[1]

A good principal leads the school improvement process. He **Diagnoses the school's strengths and weaknesses.** The principal identifies any problems with student discipline or academic learning in the school.

Communicates this information clearly to teachers, students, and parents. He explains the school's strengths and weaknesses clearly at back-to-school nights and other school events and is available at convenient hours for informal discussions with parents.

Makes school performance results readily available to parents and community members. He provides the information described in chapters 1 and 4 to any parent who asks for it. If the district doesn't make the information available, the principal gives parents good advice on what to do next.

Develops plans to improve the school. He follows the rules of good planning presented in chapter 4.

Involves parents and teachers in the school improvement planning process. He strongly encourages parents and teachers to work together on the school's improvement plan.

Develops a school budget that reflects the school's priorities. He makes a copy of this budget available to interested parents and teachers.

In working on campus plans, focus on academic standards, assessment, and accountability for results.
Leave responsibility for teaching methods to the teachers.

WHAT SHOULD I DO IF I HAVE A PROBLEM WITH MY CHILD'S TEACHER OR PRINCIPAL?

You should be concerned if your child isn't learning or if she's developing a negative attitude toward school and learning. What do you do if the teacher doesn't recognize that there's a problem or doesn't seem willing to work with you to do anything about it?

Try to identify what the problem is. Is the problem with academics or discipline? Does it involve your child, her classmates, or both? Does it seem to be confined to her classroom, or is it schoolwide? (Schoolwide problems are the principal's responsibility.) Does there seem to be a problem with the teacher's attitude toward your child? Is there a problem with her attitude toward the teacher? Is there a personality conflict between her and the teacher?

The problem may not be the teacher—it may be your child!

Talk to the teacher and make sure the problem is not due to poor communication or misunderstanding. Remember to approach him with the attitude that your goal is to help each other and to work on constructive solutions. Avoid all discussion of who is to blame. Review the principles of partnership and accountability discussed in chapter 10.

Talk to the school counselor on how to resolve the problem.

Find out what the teacher expects of your child. Is he genuinely interested in how she's doing? Does he treat her as an individual and try to help her? Does he have high expectations for her?

Visit the classroom—preferably more than once—and see for yourself what is going on. Talk to the teacher about his and the school's policy on classroom visits. Treat these visits as of equal priority with your doctor's appointments.

Find out if other problems in the classroom are affecting your child. Is the behavior of other students part of the problem? Are these problems on their way to being solved? Who is involved in trying to solve them?

Information about children other than your own must be handled
with kindness and consideration for those involved and may be
subject to legal restrictions to protect student privacy.

Jot down notes about what was said in each conversation with the teacher, so that you have a record of the effort that you and he made to help solve the problem.

Keep good records. You should be able to show
the steps that you took to resolve the problem.

If you're unable to resolve the problem by talking with the teacher and counselor, meet with the principal and let him suggest a solution. You may want to have your child moved to a different classroom. However, the principal usually has the final say on where she is placed.

If the problem is with the principal, follow the same steps as you would with the teacher: talk to the principal and work out a specific plan for resolving the problem; take notes and write a summary of what you agreed on in the meeting; and schedule a follow-up meeting or telephone conversation to make sure that each of you has kept your end of the bargain.

If you're unable to resolve the problem with the principal, talk to his supervisor, following the chain of command described in chapter 10. If you're still not satisfied, look into your options for changing schools (see chapter 4).

HOW CAN MY SCHOOL OR SCHOOL DISTRICT IMPROVE TEACHERS' EFFECTIVENESS?

The school or school district can

Hire teachers based on their skills and knowledge, not just degrees and credentials. Some degrees may tell you little about the teacher's skill or ability. But training in specific subjects can make a difference. For example, one study found that fourth-graders' reading skills improved more rapidly when their teachers had specialized training in teaching reading.[2]

Train teachers regularly, just as many companies do with their employees. Give teachers detailed information on effective methods, but don't tell them exactly how to teach. Encourage them to continue learning in the subjects they teach and also in other areas of knowledge that could increase student learning in their classrooms.

Evaluate the effectiveness of training programs by looking at student learning in the classroom. A variety of assessments of student learning should be used in these evaluations. States and school districts may also want to evaluate the programs that train beginning teachers. (See "Who Evaluates the Institutions That Train Our Teachers?")

Keep track of how well each teacher's students are learning, and take appropriate steps if problems arise.

Encourage parent participation and involvement. You help the teacher when you support your child's learning at home, participate in volunteer activities at school, encourage your child to be well behaved, and show your appreciation for the teacher when he does a good job.

WHO EVALUATES THE INSTITUTIONS THAT TRAIN OUR TEACHERS?

Does anyone evaluate colleges of education by how well their graduates do in the classroom? The colleges are accredited. Nonetheless, the short answer is no—though some large districts that hire many graduates from a college may have a good idea about the quality of its program.

In the ideal world, someone would keep track of how well the graduates of each teacher training program do in the classroom—how well their students learn—and use the information to make improvements in the program. If this issue interests you, contact your state legislator's office or state education agency to find out if anyone is looking into the idea.

Hire principals who are good at motivating teachers, supporting teacher innovation, promoting teamwork, and involving parents. An effective principal will use his leadership to get teachers and parents to work together.

Hire principals who will support teachers on disciplinary matters, and work with parents and teachers to establish clear school rules that are fairly and consistently enforced.

Give teachers the programs and supplies they need to be effective. Schools work better when good tutoring and enrichment programs are supported and when teachers don't have to waste valuable time finding enough pencils or textbooks.

Give teachers time to plan lessons and discuss effective teaching methods. Students learn more in schools where teachers talk to each other and share ideas. Planning time during the school year is scarce; one survey found that teachers work an average of fifty-six hours a week.[3]

A good time for teachers to plan, study, and learn together is when school is not in session. Your district will probably need to pay teachers to make sure this happens. To save teachers' time during the school year, the district can hire secretarial help and grading assistants for teams of teachers, as colleges do for professors.

CHECKLIST: GOOD TEACHING AND SCHOOL MANAGEMENT

What You Need to Do	Done
Treat everyone in the school with courtesy and respect.	☐
Support the teacher as he encourages your child's learning and manages the learning process.	☐
Let teachers or the principal know if there is any sign of your child having difficulty at home or at school.	☐
Write a note of appreciation to the teacher whenever he does a particularly good job. Send a copy of the note to the principal and superintendent.	☐
Write a note of appreciation to the counselor whenever he does a particularly good job. Send a copy of the note to the principal and superintendent.	☐
Write a note of appreciation whenever you see the principal doing a good job of setting priorities and communicating with parents. Send a copy to the superintendent.	☐

What You Need to Do		Done
If you have a problem with the teacher or principal, follow the appropriate steps to get the problem resolved. (See the checklist on resolving problems.)		☐
Learn about the school's or school district's training programs for teachers and principals.	Principal	☐
Support school or school district initiatives to provide meaningful training for teachers and principals.		☐
Support efforts to evaluate programs according to how well they help students learn.		☐

CHECKLIST: RESOLVING PROBLEMS

What You Need to Do	Done
Discuss the situation informally with your child and the teacher and see if you can figure out exactly what the problem is.	☐
Visit the classroom and see if you can figure out what might be causing the problem.	☐
If the problem continues, set up a meeting with the teacher to discuss the situation.	☐
Before the meeting, gather any evidence you have that would help the teacher understand the nature of the problem.	☐
Begin the meeting on a positive note before launching into a discussion of the problem. Ask about other problems that could be affecting your child.	☐
Work with the teacher to come up with a plan to solve the problem.	☐
Take notes when you speak with a teacher, staff person, or principal.	☐

What You Need to Do	Source	Done
Write a follow-up note and summarize main points and plans; send a copy of this letter to the next person in the chain of command.		☐
Keep in touch with the teacher and discuss progress. Document when the problem appears to be solved.		☐
If the problem continues, ask for a formal meeting with the teacher, principal, and counselor.		☐
If the problem continues and the teacher or principal doesn't seem interested in resolving it, look into your options for changing classrooms or schools.		☐

NOTES

1. Andrea LaRue, "The Changing Face of Teacher Tenure" (Austin: Lyndon B. Johnson School of Public Affairs, University of Texas, August 1996, professional report). This report contains a state-by-state description of teacher dismissal procedures.

2. Anecdotally, many teachers complain about how unhelpful much of their teacher training was in preparing them for day-to-day work in the classroom. *Texas Teacher Preparation Study: Interim Report 1995* (Austin: Texas Education Agency, 1995), 30-31. Private schools often do well with uncredentialed teachers. In addition, one study found that untrained laypersons did as well as credentialed teachers in educating students in social science research methods and two vocational subjects. James Popham, "Performance Tests of Teaching Proficiency: Rationale, Development, and Validation," *American Educational Research Journal* 8, no. 1 (January 1971): 105-17. A review of the research literature found no consistent relationship between additional teachers' degrees and better student learning in the classroom. See Eric Hanushek, "The Impact of Differential Expenditures on School Performance," *Issue Analysis* (Washington, D.C.: American Legislative Exchange Council, March 1990, photocopy).

However, two other studies found that, when other variables were equal, students did better in Texas and Alabama districts where more teachers had master's degrees. See Ronald Ferguson, "Paying for Public Education: New Evidence on How and Why Money Matters," *Harvard Journal on Legislation* (Summer 1991): 465-98; and Ronald Ferguson and Helen Ladd, "How and Why Money Matters: An Analysis of Alabama Schools," in Helen Ladd, ed., *Holding Schools Accountable* (Washington, D.C.: Brookings Institution, 1996), chap. 8, 265-98.

Perhaps the most plausible conclusion is that some teacher training is effective and some is not—the better reason for districts to look at what a teacher actually knows and can do.

For more on the fourth-grade reading skills study, see Omar Lopez, "The Effect of the Relationship between Classroom Student Diversity and Teacher Capacity on Student Performance" (Ph.D. diss., University of Texas at Austin, April 1995).

3. Common sense would indicate that teachers who talk to each other would share their more effective teaching methods, but there is scant research documenting this. However, research shows that teachers who work together tend to feel more effective and accountable for student learning, and this in turn contributes to student learning. Causality also runs the other way: better student learning helps teachers feel more effective and accountable. See Anthony Bryk, Eric Canburn, and Karen Louis, "Professional Community in Chicago Elementary Schools: Facilitating Factors and Organizational Consequences" (Consortium on

Chicago School Research, Chicago, 1996); Valerie Lee and J. Smith, "High School Restructuring and the Equitable Distribution of Student Achievement" (Center on Organization and Restructuring of Schools, Madison, Wis., 1995); and Valerie Lee and J. Smith, "Collective Responsibility for Learning and Its Effects on Gains in Achievement and Engagement for Early Secondary Students," *American Journal of Education* (February 1996): 103–47.

The survey of teachers' planning time, conducted by the Texas State Teachers Association, found that teachers reported spending an average of forty hours a week at school, fourteen hours a week at home preparing lessons on evenings and weekends, one hour a week calling parents, and one hour a week in meetings. A. Phillips Brooks, *Austin American-Statesman*, September 11, 1996, B1 and B3. The author has taught at the elementary level and finds the results of this survey credible from his own experience.

9

Making Incentives Work

*Students need incentives to focus on their studies,
teachers need incentives to work in teams, and
administrators need incentives to make the system
work for everyone.*

QUESTIONS ADDRESSED IN THIS CHAPTER

- Why is there interest in incentives in education?
- What are some examples of helpful and harmful incentives in education?
- What ways exist to improve incentives for students?
- What ways exist to improve incentives for parents?
- What ways exist to improve incentives for teachers and administrators?

Incentives encourage people to do things. They are rewards or penalties that favor one behavior and discourage another. Most are not financial: the approval or disapproval of other people can be a powerful motivator.

All organizations have incentives—it's important to see that they are the right ones. Good incentives

- are fair
- encourage people to do the right thing

Good incentives encourage students, teachers, and parents to "go the extra mile" for academic excellence, not just do business as usual. They help people to set the right priorities among competing uses of their time. Good incentives also support and strengthen intrinsic motivation—the inner desire to do the right thing. Intrinsic motivation is extremely important for students, teachers, administrators, and parents. However, no society or organization operates on intrinsic motivation alone.

This chapter focuses on incentives outside the classroom, provided by parents, students, school districts, colleges, employers, and society. (Teachers' use of incentives in the classroom is an issue of teaching methods, which is beyond the scope of this handbook.)

WHY IS THERE INTEREST IN INCENTIVES IN EDUCATION?

Students, parents, teachers, and administrators face too many of the wrong incentives and not enough of the right ones. Inadequate or harmful incentives might help to explain some of these distressing facts:

Many students seem to care little about their middle- and high-school education—about one-third of high-school students in one study report that they have lost interest in school, are not learning much, and get through the school day by fooling around with their classmates.[1]

> Students' intrinsic motivation to learn competes with their motivation to watch television, play video games, hang out with friends, and work longer hours for employers who pay attention to incentives.

There is a distressingly weak connection in many places between money spent in education and results accomplished, as measured by student test scores or graduation rates. Studies of the uses of new money in schools in four states found that administrators did little planning about how to use the money to achieve the greatest impact on student learning. The Kansas City, Missouri, public schools spent $34,000 per student as part of a court order and had little improvement to show in the students' reading and mathematics skills.[2]

Educators are often slow to learn from each other. Often, there is little communication among teachers, administrators, and researchers about what actually works. Effective programs sometimes exist alongside ineffective ones, and ineffective educators often do not find out what their neighbors are doing right.[3]

WHAT ARE EXAMPLES OF HELPFUL AND HARMFUL INCENTIVES IN EDUCATION?

Helpful incentives encourage
- **students to study hard** and take pride in high academic achievement
- **parents to spend time** with their children, attend school activities and teacher conferences, and help their children be successful
- **teachers to share information** about what works best in the classroom and spend additional time learning while school is not in session
- **teachers to work with difficult students** in high-poverty areas and learn about programs and methods that work with those students
- **the best students to enter teaching as a profession, and the best teachers to stay in the profession**
- **administrators to operate schools where student learning has the highest priority**
- **administrators to focus on effective long-term solutions,** not on popular but ineffective educational fads

Harmful incentives encourage
- **students to pressure their classmates not to study.** High-school teachers may create those incentives when they grade students based on their performance relative to others in the class.[4] A student can improve his class rank in two ways: study harder or convince his classmates to study less. Which is easier?
- **parents to spend less time with their children and be less involved with their children's schools.** Employers create these incentives when they pressure employees to work long

hours and deny them time off to attend teacher conferences and other important school events.

- **teachers to leave high-poverty schools.** School districts create these incentives when they give low priority to improving schools in high-poverty areas and to encouraging parent involvement in those schools.
- **administrators not to remove burned-out teachers and principals.** State laws and district policies create these incentives when they make it difficult to dismiss teachers or principals who are doing a poor job.
- **administrators to inflate test scores** by excluding students from testing, encouraging test-coaching, and adopting tests that are too easy. Parents, school board members, and journalists create these incentives when they pay lots of attention to test scores but little attention to how the numbers are produced, how accurate they are, or what level of student learning they represent (see chapter 3).

WHAT WAYS EXIST TO IMPROVE INCENTIVES FOR STUDENTS?

Give your child more personal attention and show interest in what he is learning. The more attention he receives—especially on his schoolwork—the more motivated he's likely to be. This is why many middle- and high-school students thrive in schools where they receive personal coaching from teachers.

Discourage your high-schooler from working during the school year. His education is more important, and he can gain needed work experience while school is not in session. As an alternative, allow him to work only if he takes challenging courses and keeps his grades up in school.

Working during the school year can be appropriate if the work is directly related to your child's academic program—for example, a student studying health care might hold a job in a medical lab.

Avoid "incentive inflation." When your child is rewarded regardless of performance, then the reward is meaningless.

Schools and colleges can base academic recognition on students' performance relative to a set standard, not to other students. This way, students no longer benefit by encouraging their classmates to neglect their schoolwork. In fact, a studious classmate can become an asset to his fellow students. This effect is strengthened if groups of students receive recognition for the performance of the group.

States and school districts can raise the standards for high-school graduation. This has already been done in many states, although the standards are still low. Many states require students to demonstrate no more than an eighth-grade proficiency level to graduate. Schools can also give advanced diplomas to students who meet higher standards.

Colleges can dedicate a greater share of their scholarship money to low- and moderate-income students who do well in advanced courses in high school. Students who pass Advanced Placement tests can save on college costs by placing out of college courses.

Colleges can deny college credit toward graduation for remedial work done in college. This provides an incentive for students to prepare for college before they get there.

Employers can offer better entry-level jobs to students who do well in school. Schools should provide student transcripts to employers quickly on request, and they should represent true accomplishment, not grade inflation.

WHAT WAYS EXIST TO IMPROVE INCENTIVES FOR PARENTS?

Your employer can create more part-time and flex-time job opportunities and reduce the economic penalty you pay for spending time with your children.

Your employer can give you time off to attend important school events. Labor laws in California protect employees' right to take off four hours a year per child to visit their children's schools.[5]

Your child's school, your employer, and other local businesses can publicly thank you when your child does well in school or shows remarkable improvement and when you volunteer at school.

WHAT WAYS EXIST TO IMPROVE INCENTIVES FOR TEACHERS AND ADMINISTRATORS?

There are three basic kinds of incentives for teachers and administrators:

Incentives arising from public information about schools. For example, if the newspapers report that students at Jones Middle School are doing exceptionally well, this can get parents and teachers interested in making those results happen in other schools.

Systems of rewards and sanctions created by states or school districts. States and school districts can reward teachers and administrators for getting better training, taking on more difficult assignments, or doing a better job. They can let go teachers or principals in schools where students aren't learning.

Incentives created by market competition, as when schools compete with each other to attract students, or groups of teachers or private management companies compete with superintendents for the right to manage schools.

Here are specific ways that the school or school district can improve incentives for educators:

Pay teachers more for training that makes a difference in the classroom. Unfortunately, much teacher training doesn't, so it's important to keep track of what works.

Give teachers in low-income schools the pay and working conditions needed to get them to stay. Make parent involvement a priority in those schools—parent support is important for teachers' effectiveness and morale.[6]

Recognize and reward teachers and administrators who do an excellent job. If your own teacher does an excellent job in the classroom, be sure to let her know that you appreciate her work. Write a note to the principal saying what a good job she does.

Provide better information to you and the public about how well each school and school district is doing. If a school has an excellent group of eighth-grade mathematics teachers, the rest of the world should know about it. This requires an assessment system that focuses on academic gain, compares how schools do with equally prepared students, and is resistant to test score inflation (see chapters 3 and 4).

Encourage the creation of new schools that can compete with existing ones. Encourage parents and teachers to create new magnet, charter, or private schools to try out new teaching methods or serve students with special interests or needs. In East Harlem, for example, public-school teachers created 31 small new magnet schools in the existing school buildings. By early 1997, 480 charter schools had been created in sixteen states in the District of Columbia, and proposals for many others were on the drawing board.[7]

Allow open enrollment and flexible transfer policies to enable parents to decide which public school best meets their child's needs. As of 1996, sixteen states had policies allowing students to enroll their children in any public school district in the state.[8]

CHECKLIST: INCENTIVES

What You Need to Do	Done
Understand why incentives are important even when everyone has good intentions.	☐
Understand that incentives help people to set priorities when many activities compete for the use of their time.	☐
Understand that some of the most important incentives do not involve material rewards.	☐
Understand the difference between extrinsic and intrinsic motivation.	☐
Understand the characteristics of good incentives.	☐
Identify incentives in your child's school or community that	☐
• encourage learning and academic achievement,	☐
• discourage learning and academic achievement.	☐
Make a list of the incentives you use at home and mark them as positive or negative: emphasize the positive ones!	☐

What You Need to Do	Done
Ask your child what makes him want to do his best work. Find ways to do what motivates him.	☐
Make a list of the incentives in your life that	☐
• encourage you to focus on your child's education,	☐
• discourage you from focusing on your child's education.	☐
Think of additional ways to spend more time with your child.	☐
Understand the three basic kinds of incentives for teachers and administrators.	☐
Support helpful incentives and speak out against harmful ones.	☐

NOTES

1. Steinberg, *Beyond the Classroom*, 71.

2. See Hanushek, "The Impact of Differential Expenditures." Hanushek's results have been misinterpreted to mean that "money makes no difference," but actually he argues that money has been badly spent in many places and thus hasn't made a *strong* and *consistent* difference.

One example occurred when the Austin, Texas, school district gave sixteen "priority schools" in low-income areas an average of $500 extra per student between 1989 and 1994. Two of these schools emphasized parental involvement and new teaching methods and had dramatic results to show for the money; fourteen schools did not and had little to show. The average impact of extra money over the sixteen schools was small, but that average hides the fact that additional money was highly effective where it was well spent. See Richard Murnane and Frank Levy, "Why Money Matters Sometimes," *Education Week* (September 11, 1996): 48 and 36.

For an analysis that indicates that money makes a difference, see Larry Hedges, Richard Laine, and Rob Greenwald, "Does Money Matter? A Meta-Analysis of Studies of the Effects of Differential School Inputs on Student Outcomes," *Educational Researcher* (April 1994): 5–14.

For a summary of the research on the uses of new money, see Allan Odden and William Clune, "Improving Educational Productivity and School Finance," Educational Researcher 24, no. 9 (December 1995): 6–10.

"The Cash Street Kids," *Economist* (August 28, 1993): 23–25. The Kansas City schools were given access to over a billion dollars in state money as part of a desegregation order, to spend enough money on magnet schools to attract white students from the suburbs. Most of the money was spent on new school buildings. Since the academics didn't improve, few students were attracted from the suburbs.

3. For example, one effective program to teach mathematical skills to elementary school children, the SEED program (for "special early education for the disadvantaged"), has been around since the late 1960s but is little noticed by educators. Educators in one elementary school in Houston, Texas, that was effective at teaching reading to low-income black students were told by administrators that their teaching methods were not appropriate. Author's conversation with Thaddeus Lott, principal, Wesley Elementary School, November 1993.

Lack of teacher preparation time may contribute to the problem. School district policymakers may need incentives to budget more preparation time for teachers, and some teachers may need encouragement to change their approach when students aren't learning.

4. Colleges create the same harmful incentives when they admit students or offer scholarships based on class rank.

5. Section 230.8 of the California Labor Code states that "no employer, who employs 25 or more employees working at the same location, shall discharge or in any way discriminate against an employee who is a parent or guardian of any child in kindergarten or grades 1 to 12, inclusive, for taking off four hours each school year, per child, to visit the school of the child, if the employee, prior to taking the time off, gives reasonable notice to the employer of the planned absence of the employee."

6. In many areas, the low-income schools are populated by the least experienced teachers, because that's where they can find jobs. As soon as the teachers acquire skill and experience, they move out to teach in the more affluent areas where parental involvement is usually greater and the pay is often higher.

7. For more on the East Harlem example, see Sy Fliegal, *Miracle in East Harlem: The Fight for Choice in Public Education* (New York, 1993).

For information on the District of Columbia case, see *National Charter School Directory* (Washington, D.C.: Center for Education Reform, 1997). Order through CER's Web page, available from http://edreform.com/publicat.htm.

8. The states with open enrollment were Arizona, Arkansas, California, Colorado, Delaware, Idaho, Iowa, Massachusetts, Minnesota, Nebraska, New Hampshire, North Dakota, Ohio, Tennessee, Utah, and Washington. Parents may, however, find that the most desirable schools and school districts have "no space available." This is a reason for policies encouraging teachers to create new schools. Center for Education Reform state-by-state summary of school reform, available from http://edreform.com/pubs/edstats.htm.

10

Improving Accountability in Education

The buck stops here.
— sign on the desk of President Harry S Truman, 1948

QUESTIONS ADDRESSED IN THIS CHAPTER

- What are some of my responsibilities as a parent?
- How can I tell if teachers and principals are responsible for what they should be?
- What are accountability systems?
- How can parents and educators be more accountable to each other?
- How can I hold teachers and principals accountable?

Who is responsible, or accountable, for the education of our children? **As a parent, you hold the primary responsibility for your child's education**—although you delegate some responsibility to the teacher when your child goes to school and she takes on increasing responsibility as she gets older.

Accountability means "responsibility for results." **Accountable people take responsibility for getting results and enlist the help of others along the way.**

Students who are accountable don't say, "I have a bad teacher, therefore I can't learn the material." Instead they say, "I'm going to learn the material, even if I have to get tutoring."

Parents who are accountable don't say, "Neither my child nor her teachers listen to me, so I can't get her to learn." They say, "I'm going to figure out a way to get her to learn."

Teachers and administrators who are accountable don't say, "The students and their parents aren't cooperating, so we can't get these students to learn." They say, "We're going to find a way to reach these students and their parents."

On a baseball team, all of the players are jointly responsible for the result: winning the game. In addition, each player has the separate responsibility to play his or her position. Likewise in education, parents, educators, and students are jointly responsible for student learning, but each "player" has separate responsibilities as well. Every school or school district should be able to describe clearly what those responsibilities are.

WHAT ARE SOME OF MY RESPONSIBILITIES AS A PARENT?

In working with the school, your responsibilities are to

Make sure your child does well academically. Let her know that her schoolwork is her most important job. Know what she is expected to learn, and work with her at home to make sure that she learns it. Make sure she attends classes and finishes and returns her homework. Attend teacher conferences and communicate regularly with the teacher. Organize family activities around school hours so that she does not miss any school days unless she's sick.

Make sure that she does not have behavior problems at school. See that she knows and understands the school's rules and the consequences for breaking them. Emphasize to her the importance of sticking by the rules, and support the school's right to correct her if she misbehaves.

Take good care of her. Make sure she gets plenty of sleep on school nights. Send her to school clean, healthy, and well fed. Make sure she gets to school on time every day. Make sure she has regular medical and dental checkups and follow the doctor's advice.

Teach her how to become a successful adult. Spend time with your child and teach her important values, such as honesty and respect for other people. Teach her to be responsible and make good choices. Don't let television or other children take your place as her teacher.

Your child's teacher should provide you with a clear
description of your and your child's responsibilities.

HOW CAN I TELL IF TEACHERS AND PRINCIPALS ARE RESPONSIBLE FOR WHAT THEY SHOULD BE?

Here are some questions you can ask:

- What do teachers and principals say they are accountable for? Do they act in a way that is consistent with their statements?
- If the school isn't safe, who accepts responsibility for this situation?
- If the students aren't learning as much as they should, who accepts responsibility for this situation?

See chapter 8 for a more detailed discussion of the responsibilities of teachers and principals.

WHAT ARE ACCOUNTABILITY SYSTEMS?

Some states and school districts have developed accountability systems to hold educators and students responsible for educational results. Good accountability systems are rules, policies, or practices that

Assign responsibilities so that students, parents, teachers, and administrators know who is responsible for what.

Establish high academic standards that are attainable and clearly explained to students, parents, educators, and the general public.

Assess student learning in a variety of ways that measure and report student improvement, or gains, as well as levels of knowledge and skill—this is necessary to judge school effectiveness. The assessments should show whether students are reaching high academic standards and should use a variety of methods to reduce the risk of test score inflation. (See chapter 3.)

Inform parents and the public how students in the school or district are doing and which schools are most effective. The reports should describe student progress over time and compare schools' success in educating specific student populations—for example, students who are academically advanced when they enter the school.

Provide consequences tied to student learning. For example, students who don't learn may find themselves without a high-school diploma; principals in schools where students don't learn may find themselves looking for another job.

It's important to understand two things about accountability systems:

Clear, accurate, complete information is the most important product of any accountability system. Because good systems have nothing to hide, this might be called the Sunlight Principle of Accountability. Accurate public information on student gains and school effectiveness encourages educators in the less effective schools to learn from the more effective ones.

Poor information can lead to perverse incentives. If it's easy to inflate test scores by narrow forms of "teaching to the test," then educators will have an incentive to do so. If average test score levels—not gains—are the only school performance measure used, then teachers will have incentives to leave high-poverty schools for schools in affluent areas, where students start out ahead.

HOW CAN PARENTS AND EDUCATORS BE MORE ACCOUNTABLE TO EACH OTHER?

In an accountable school parents, teachers, and administrators are partners, and partners are accountable to each other. Your child's teacher and principal should treat you as a partner in the education of your child.

What do partners owe each other?

Good communication. Partners express clearly what each expects of the other. If there is a problem, they sit down and discuss it with the emphasis on finding solutions, not debating whose fault the problem was.

Mutual respect. Partners treat each other as equals, listen respectfully to each other's ideas, build trust with each other, and do not intimidate each other.

Joint planning. Partners plan together to achieve common goals. Your child's teacher should be eager to work with you on a learning plan. Her principal should encourage you to participate in the school improvement planning process.

An emphasis on results. Although you may share ideas on teaching methods with the teacher, and the teacher may share parenting tips with you, each of you is responsible for deciding how to do his own job best. Your child's teacher is not accountable for using one particular method of teaching reading—he is accountable for teaching your child how to read. Focus on what your child is learning, not the methods used by the teacher.

HOW CAN I HOLD TEACHERS AND PRINCIPALS ACCOUNTABLE?

What can I do if my child's teacher or principal isn't doing his job and doesn't follow these four rules of good partnership?

Be a good partner yourself. Express clearly what you want, treat the teacher or principal respectfully, work together on a plan, and focus on results.

Keep good records. You should be able to show, in case anyone asks, that you made a strong effort to work with the teacher or principal. What meetings did you have, and what did you agree on? What were you unable to agree on? Who followed through with his part of the agreement? Did you set goals for your child? Which of these were accomplished?

Focus on policies, not personnel. Remember that you don't hire and fire teachers—the principal or other school officials do. You don't hire principals—the superintendent does (in a private school, the school's board of directors hires the principal or headmaster). The school and district should have policies in place to hold teachers and principals accountable. What are these policies? Are they any good? Are they written down? If so, can you have a copy? Are they being followed? What are the principal and superintendent doing to make sure that the policies are followed?

The school should be able to show you a written
copy of any school or school district policy.

Follow the chain of command. If the principal won't enforce
school or school district policies, go to his boss—the area director or
the superintendent. If the superintendent won't enforce the policies—or if the policies are inadequate—go to the school board (see
"Chain of Command in a Large School District").

CHAIN OF COMMAND IN A LARGE SCHOOL DISTRICT

In a large school district, the chain of command probably looks
like this. You should begin with the teacher.

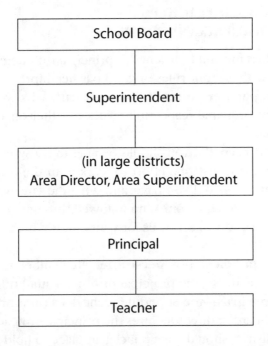

In a small school district, the chain of command would go
straight from principal to superintendent. In private schools, the
chain of command goes from teacher to school director or headmaster, to the school's board of directors. Find out the chain of
command in your school or school district.

The school board's job is to set school district policies, decide on the budget, hire the superintendent, and make sure that the superintendent follows the district's policies. School board members are elected and can be held accountable by you and other members of the public for setting good policies.

Remember that there's strength in numbers. Principals, superintendents, and school boards are more likely to respond to a group of fifteen or twenty concerned parents working together to change a policy than to one concerned parent working alone.

CHECKLIST: ACCOUNTABILITY

What You Need to Do	Source	Done
Understand your responsibilities as a parent.		☐
Understand your child's responsibilities and how these increase as she gets older.		
Find out what the school holds you and your child responsible for.	Teacher	☐
Find out what teachers and the principal say they are responsible for.	Teachers, principal	☐
Find out who takes responsibility at the school when something goes wrong or is not working.		☐
Ask for information about the school's academic performance and learn how easy it is to get it.	Principal, district office	☐
Find out about your state's or school district's accountability system:	State, school district	
• who is responsible for what?		☐
• how high are the academic standards?		☐
• how is student learning assessed?		☐

What You Need to Do	Source	Done
• how is school success evaluated?		☐
• how are student learning and school success reported?		☐
• what happens if students don't learn?		☐
Learn the rules of good partnership and apply them with your child's teacher and principal.		☐
Learn what to do if others do not apply these rules. (See the checklist on and keeping a partner accountable.)		☐

CHECKLIST: KEEPING A PARTNER ACCOUNTABLE

What You Need to Do	Source	Done
Be a good partner yourself: Communicate clearly, treat others respectfully, work together on a plan, and focus on results.		☐
Document your efforts to work with the teacher or principal. Write down what you discussed, what you agreed on, and what you were unable to agree on.		☐
Document whether each of you followed through on what you agreed to do.		☐
Focus on policies, not personnel. Get a copy of the school or school district policies related to your concern.		☐
Follow the chain of command. If you have trouble working with the teacher, talk to the principal. If you can't work with the principal, talk to his boss. If you have no luck with the district administration, appeal to the school board.		☐
Work with other parents if the problem affects many students, not just your child.		☐

11

Getting Involved

You are your child's first teacher.

QUESTIONS ADDRESSED IN THIS CHAPTER

- What can I do at home to help my child succeed in school?
- How can I help my child learn from homework?
- How can I work successfully with my child's school?
- What can teachers and the principal do to help parents get involved?
- What can I do if educators do not seem to want parents to be involved?
- How can I attract community donations and volunteers to my school?
- How can assistance for schools be tied to specific goals?
- How can parents get involved in their school's improvement planning process?
- How can parents get involved in the academic improvement planning process for their local school district?

You have more power over your child's education than his teachers do. Consider the following story told by a Texas first-grade teacher. One child in her class came to school with the message from home that "school is stupid." He could barely count to ten. Another child came to first grade discussing the use of explosive bolts to separate the stages of the Saturn V rocket.[1] This example shows the difference that parents make at home.

By paying close attention to your child's learning at home and working closely with his school, you can make sure that he gets a first-rate education.

WHAT CAN I DO AT HOME TO HELP
MY CHILD SUCCEED IN SCHOOL?

Let your child know that his learning is Priority Number One. Learning comes ahead of working after school, watching television, or socializing with friends. For your part, pay close attention to his schoolwork, go to teacher conferences, attend important school events, and find time to volunteer at the school.

Provide a stable, secure home environment. Many children have trouble at school because they're struggling at home. A home should be a safe place, where your child can easily study and recharge for the next school day.

Establish routines and rules for behavior at home. By giving your child a say in the decision-making process, you can hold him accountable for following the rules.

> "Elizabeth, as we agreed, we're going to turn the television off after dinner so that you can concentrate on your homework and have time to read before your 9:00 bedtime."

> "William, a good place for you to do your homework is at the kitchen table. We'll make sure there's no noise to bother you, and I'll be there to help you if you need it."

Show interest in what your child is learning.

> "Michael, let's take turns reading to each other every night before you go to bed. I like to hear you read stories."

> "Alex, you did a wonderful job on this math assignment! I'd like to put it up on the refrigerator."

> "Laura, tell me what you're doing in science. Do you like your class? What new things have you learned about? Would you like to take chemistry next year in high school?"

Plan after-school supervision for him. After-school activities give him opportunities to socialize with friends without interfering with his schoolwork. They also provide structure for latchkey children.

Get to know the parents of his friends and talk to them on a regular basis. This allows you to form a close group and share information about the school and students.

Be aware of what your child's friends are doing: he is likely to be doing the same things.

Find out from his teachers what you can do at home to help him learn.

Provide enrichment activities, for example, a museum children's class, a visit to the planetarium, or a weekend trip to a historical town.

The teacher should give you a list of your child's responsibilities—for example, how many days a week he will be expected to do homework—and provide descriptions of activities that are good for learning.

HOW CAN I HELP MY CHILD LEARN FROM HOMEWORK?

Most homework assignments help your child review at home what he has already learned at school. Some assignments also help him learn new information from books, encyclopedias, or the Internet.

Find out the teacher's and school's homework policy at the beginning of the year. How often will homework be assigned? In what subjects? How many minutes a day should your child be spending on homework?

Set aside a quiet place and time for your child to study. As much as possible, homework should be part of a regular routine: for example, 7:00 P.M. is "homework time."

Check his homework, but don't do it for him. Find out if he understands what he is supposed to do and knows how to get started. For example, what's the first thing to do on a writing assignment or an algebra word problem? Write a note to the teacher if he has great difficulty doing the assignment and doesn't seem to know the material.

Check his homework assignments even if he finishes them at school. He needs to know that you think his work is important, and you need to know what he's learning.

If he needs to memorize information, such as the multiplication table, have him practice a few minutes every day. Quiz him for a few minutes in the car. At home, have him cover up the item to be memorized, say it, uncover it, say it again, write it down, cover up his writing, and say it again. Have him memorize the information a little bit at a time. Ask your teacher to teach him tricks for memorizing information. Allow plenty of time for him to memorize information—"crammed" information is easily forgotten.

If your child is asked to memorize words and formulas in such a
content area as science, make sure he understands the concepts
as well. Can he explain the same idea in other words?
Can he give examples? Can he describe how the idea is applied?

Help him get organized to finish projects and papers on time. Have him break the project into parts and work out a schedule for completing each part. By when should he complete the background reading? do the outline or design? purchase any necessary materials? conduct the experiment? complete the first draft? write the final version?

Have him plan to finish ahead of the deadline. This allows extra time in case the assignment takes longer than planned and gives him a chance to enjoy being done while his classmates are still struggling to complete the assignment.

If you have a question on how much you should help him, ask the teacher. Some teachers encourage parents to call attention to mistakes: "Take another look at problem 9." "Can you check the punctuation in the second sentence?"Ask your teacher for guidelines on how best to help him with writing assignments, math problems, or science projects. (See "How to Help Your Child When You Don't Know the Subject Yourself.")

HOW TO HELP YOUR CHILD WHEN YOU DON'T KNOW THE SUBJECT YOURSELF

Here's what can you do if your child is studying algebra or ancient history and your own knowledge of the subject is rusty:

- Show enthusiasm for your child's learning and for learning new things yourself.
- Have him explain what he has learned. If he can "play teacher" and help you understand the subject, he probably understands it well himself.
- Make sure he does his homework and provide a quiet place and regular time for him to study every night.
- Have him write down questions for the teacher if he has trouble understanding the material. The next night, find out about the answers that the teacher supplied.
- Get help if he continues to have trouble. Find out from the teacher or counselor how he can get tutoring in the subject.

HOW CAN I WORK SUCCESSFULLY WITH MY CHILD'S SCHOOL?

Get to know your child's teachers and principal. Talk to the teacher regularly about your child's progress.

Understand the school's academic expectations. What is he expected to learn over the next six or nine weeks? What will he be learning later this year? Is he making adequate progress? (See chapters 1 and 2 to find out how he's doing and what he should be learning.)

Understand the school's disciplinary expectations. What are the teacher's and school's rules, and what are the consequences for breaking them? Does your child understand these rules and consequences?

Volunteer at school. Help teachers in the classroom by reading to students or helping to make materials for lessons. Share your expertise with the school by teaching a class. Participate in the parent-teacher organization, as well as other school activities. If you work full-time during the week, ask the teacher how you can help on evenings and weekends.

When you volunteer at school, you learn more about what goes on there and your child will take pride in your involvement.

Stay involved as he gets older. Older students still need guidance and support from adults. Encourage other parents to stay involved, too. The more you and other parents are involved at the school, the less embarrassing it is for your child when you show up. (See "Children of Involved Parents Do Better in High School.")

Find out what your local parent-teacher organization (PTO or PTA) is doing and work with them on ways to help students.

CHILDREN OF INVOLVED PARENTS DO BETTER IN HIGH SCHOOL

When Parents Do More ...	Their Children Have ...
Involvement at home	
Discussing current school experiences	Higher grades and test scores
Enrolling student in music class outside of school	Higher grades and test scores
Restricting television viewing	Higher test scores
Supervising after-school activities	Higher grades and test scores
Planning with child for high school	Higher grades

When Parents Do More ...	Their Children Have ...
Involvement at school	
Contacting school about academic matters	Higher test scores
Volunteering at school	Higher grades
Participating in PTA/PTO	Higher grades
Involvement in the community	
Having parent friendship networks	Higher grades and test scores[2]

WHAT CAN TEACHERS AND THE PRINCIPAL DO TO HELP PARENTS GET INVOLVED?

Make you feel welcome when you visit the school. A "Parents and Visitors Are Welcome" sign is posted on the front door. They greet you warmly when you enter the school office. The school has a place where parents can meet and provides books on child development, education, and parenting. The school holds parent-teacher lunches or evening meetings often and gives tours to new families coming into the school.

Let you know they are interested in your opinions. Teachers and principals welcome opportunities to speak with parents—simply make an appointment. If you're meeting about a problem with your child, the teacher or principal listens carefully to your concerns and your suggestions and works with you to resolve the problem. If you're concerned about a problem at the school, you're encouraged to join a parent-teacher committee to discuss solutions to the problem.

Speak clearly to you in language that you understand. The teacher and principal explain things to you in everyday language, not educational jargon. If you have a friend who does not speak English, the school makes an interpreter—who could be a parent volunteer— available at meetings that parent attends.

Educators have their own language regarding education, just as doctors do regarding health. It may take several tries to get a clear answer or explanation, but be persistent. It's worth it!

Suggest several ways in which you can help. The school makes a variety of volunteer activities available for you.

Be available for you during convenient hours. The school has programs, events, and volunteer activities available in the evening or on weekends for parents who work.

When teachers and administrators are open to parent involvement and communicate well with parents, students are likely to do better. (See "How Parent Involvement Can Benefit Students.")

Ask the school for a list of suggested ways you can get involved.

HOW PARENT INVOLVEMENT CAN BENEFIT STUDENTS

In Austin, Texas, in early 1991, a new school principal in a low-income neighborhood gathered parents and teachers together to discuss the state of the school. Some parents were surprised to learn that the school's test scores were second lowest in the city. "We thought all the kids were doing well," commented one startled parent.[3]

The principal and teachers worked with Austin Interfaith, a local community organizing group, to help parents and other neighborhood residents get involved. With parental support, the teachers adopted the district's gifted and talented curriculum as the standard for all students. The school received funding for a clinic to address the children's health problems and began a Young Scientists' Academy for sixth-grade students. Parents also became more involved in decision-making at the school: they even sat on committees to hire new teachers.

In three years, the pass rate on the state achievement test by the school's fifth-graders rose from 12 to 69 percent. The school went from having 50 percent of its teachers transfer elsewhere in a single year to no teacher turnover. The principal attributed these gains to increased parental involvement.[4] Certainly the principal's willingness to talk frankly about the problems of the school helped as well.

WHAT CAN I DO IF EDUCATORS DO NOT
SEEM TO WANT PARENTS TO BE INVOLVED?

Teachers and administrators may resist parent involvement for several reasons:

Teachers legitimately do not want parents telling them how to do their jobs. Respect the training, experience, and knowledge of the teacher. It's important to keep your main attention on *results*—what your child is learning—and not on the *methods* the teacher uses to teach him. If the results aren't there, then work with the teacher to develop a plan to change the situation.

Educators may be wary of criticism from parents. They may not realize that parents are potentially their strongest allies. Let them know that you are interested in helping and working in partnership with them. Let them know that you appreciate their work.

Educators may not know how to use parents' energies to help their school. Have a list of ways in which you are willing to help out. For instance, you may want to read to or tutor some of the students during the week or help organize a Saturday art program. In addition, emphasize your readiness to help your child meet the school's academic and disciplinary expectations.

Educators may have difficulty communicating with parents. Be persistent; don't be afraid to ask questions, sometimes repeatedly, when you don't understand something. Chances are, other parents don't understand either. You will do everyone a favor by asking for a clearer explanation.

Educators may not speak the parents' native language. If one of your friends does not speak English and the teacher cannot understand her native language, ask the school principal to find someone who can talk to her. As a second resort, call the main number of the school district and find out who in the district speaks the language.

What can you do if you encounter problems?

Be polite and respectful. Ask "How can I help? What do you suggest?" instead of "Why don't you know how to teach?"

Explain to the teacher the expectations you have for your child and the school, and ask what expectations she has for

your child. "Ms. Garza, I expect Rebecca to do her very best and complete all of her assignments on time. Sometimes she has trouble with homework. It would be very helpful if you would send home clear instructions and an example of what she needs to do, so that I can help her."

Be persistent. Don't give up. Someone out there will listen and help you change things.

Don't let anyone brush you off. Examples of responses to watch for are:

- "Thanks for offering to help, but I just don't have much for you to do."
- "Let's sit on that idea for a while."
- "You're the only parent who has ever raised that issue."

Be sure to follow the proper chain of command.

1. Start with your child's teacher and try to resolve the problem.
2. If the problem is not solved with the teacher, meet with the principal.
3. If the principal doesn't solve the problem, meet with her boss.
4. As a last resort, take the problem to the school board.

Remember that there's strength in numbers. As we pointed out in chapter 10, a group of parents are more likely to get a problem addressed than is one parent working alone.

> Complaining about the school is not nearly as effective
> as challenging the school to meet an ambitious but
> attainable goal. Rather than "Our school isn't teaching children
> to read," ask "Can we get every student to read third-grade
> books or better by the middle of third grade? Can we
> work together on a plan to make this happen?"

HOW CAN I ATTRACT COMMUNITY DONATIONS AND VOLUNTEERS TO MY SCHOOL?

Many community groups may be willing to help your child's school with donations of money, supplies, and volunteer hours. How can the school attract these donations?

Identify likely donors. These will be different for every community. Your Chamber of Commerce may have a list of groups that might be willing to help. Retired citizen organizations may be a good source of volunteers to work with individual students.

Identify the needs of the school and actively solicit assistance from community organizations to meet those needs.

Show the donors that the school has a plan to put their donations to good use.

Identify additional resources the school must find to make best use of outside donations. If volunteer tutoring time is donated, the school must find someone to schedule the meetings between tutors and students. If computers and software are donated, the school must find someone to train the teachers in their use.

Document what the assistance accomplished. If possible, publish the results, perhaps by way of a newspaper article or newsletter. Donors, especially commercial ones, appreciate seeing their names in print, since it's good public relations and free advertising. This may also get you repeat donations.

Publicly thank the donors and volunteers. The key word here is "publicly." It's important that volunteers feel that their work is recognized and that the whole community know that assistance to the school is appreciated.

HOW CAN ASSISTANCE FOR SCHOOLS BE TIED TO SPECIFIC GOALS?

Community or PTO/PTA assistance will do more good if it's targeted to the specific needs of the school and if donors and the school keep track of what was accomplished.

Assistance can be divided into three categories based on how carefully it's targeted and how closely the results are monitored.

General assistance consists of money or supplies donated to a school, without a plan about how the school might best use the donation. This is easy for the donor but can be difficult for the school, especially when the donation comes in the form of supplies that the school doesn't know how to use. The results from this type of assistance can be difficult to document.

Targeted assistance is designed to meet a specific school need. For example, a group of parents and business leaders might raise money to hire a Spanish teacher for the school. In this case, it's possible to document *where* the donation helped but not *how much* it helped.

Goal-based assistance not only identifies a need—such as improving students' reading or Spanish skills—but also sets specific goals and evaluates afterward whether the goals were met. The goal of hiring a Spanish teacher might be to bring 120 third- and fourth-grade students up to a certain level of proficiency. After a year or two, the donor and school can evaluate whether the goal has been accomplished. This documents *how much* the donation helped, showing whether it was a good investment. (See "How Goal-Based Assistance Might Work in Your Child's School.")

HOW GOAL-BASED ASSISTANCE MIGHT WORK IN YOUR CHILD'S SCHOOL

Suppose teachers in your child's school have identified ten second-grade students who are a year behind in reading and need to be caught up by the end of third grade.

Based on the experience of other schools, the school's planning committee estimates that this will take an average of sixty hours of one-to-one tutoring per student, plus twenty hours of training of the third-grade teachers and the commitment of time to do three home visits to each of the children's parents. Teachers in the school identify two reading assessments that will be used at the end to determine whether the students have reached the goal.

After identifying what the assistance will cost, your committee begins the search for donors. If you find only half of the resources that you need, the school has the choice of lowering the expected goal or finding a way to accomplish the same goal with fewer resources.

At the end of the year, the school tests the students' reading ability and learns that seven of the ten students have met the goal. Based on that information, the school develops a plan to assist the other three students in the following year.

HOW CAN PARENTS GET INVOLVED IN THEIR SCHOOL'S IMPROVEMENT PLANNING PROCESS?

Ask the principal how planning for school improvement is done at your child's school and how parents can participate in the process.

Suggest to all who will listen that parent involvement in school planning is a good way to inform parents about the school's goals, and gain their support for the school's academic and disciplinary policies. Parent involvement can also make it easier for the school to raise money, as many private schools have found. Even if parents themselves can't contribute much money, many have employers and other contacts who can.

Identify the school's academic strengths and weaknesses. Use test score information and the opinions of parents and teachers to identify these areas (see chapter 4).

Review the school's plan for improvement. Remember the principles of good planning (discussed in chapter 4) when evaluating the school's improvement plan: it should establish specific, measurable goals; identify steps that are likely to take the school from here to there; estimate the time and money required; establish a timetable and responsibilities for carrying out the plan; and describe how to monitor progress and know when the goals are accomplished.

Work with teachers and the principal to pick one or two priority areas for improvement. For example, an elementary school's improvement plan might focus on writing in the early grades. A middle or high school's improvement plan might concentrate on getting students to take more advanced math courses.

Listen carefully and respectfully, and take time to do your homework. If the school is considering adopting a new reading program, for example, be prepared to study evidence on whether this reading program works.[5]

Ask for regular reports on the school's progress toward reaching its goals. Remember that the methods teachers use are not as important as their ability to show that they are producing the desired results.

> Your school's parent-teacher organization can encourage its members to get involved in the school improvement planning process and coordinate fundraising and volunteer activities to help the school reach its goals. An ambitious PTO/PTA might also get involved in districtwide plannin.

HOW CAN PARENTS GET INVOLVED IN THE ACADEMIC IMPROVEMENT PLANNING PROCESS FOR THEIR LOCAL SCHOOL DISTRICT?

Combine numbers, persistence, and clear goals, with the latter two being most important. Five or ten well-organized, persistent, and focused parents can make a difference. (See "How to Demonstrate Numbers, Persistence, and Clear Goals.")

Get four or more people together as a group. Your elected school board is responsible for setting policies and priorities for the local school district. They adopt the budget, hire the superintendent, and adopt academic and disciplinary policies for the district. Most school board meetings are attended by the same few people every time. Under these circumstances, any organized group of parents who show up in force—especially if they attend more than one meeting—will make a strong impression.

HOW TO DEMONSTRATE NUMBERS, PERSISTENCE, AND CLEAR GOALS

Clear goals: Start with one or two specific, measurable, attainable goals for your school district. You might pick three or four goals, and decide which one to work on first.

Numbers: Find out how many people come to the typical school board meeting. Choose a meeting date where the agenda doesn't have anything of great interest to a large group of people and show up with enough of your friends to triple the size of the crowd. Call each school board member ahead of time to let them know you are coming and to explain what your group's agenda is.

Persistence: Show persistence by staying around and working on the same issue for more than a single school year. Develop a two- or five-year plan to work for your group's main goal. Meet with the education reporter of the local newspaper monthly to keep her up to date on your group's and the district's progress. Have two or three supporters of your group attend school board meetings once a month to give a two-minute talk on progress toward accomplishing the goal.[6]

Include teachers in your group. They have knowledge that your group needs. Good teachers have a practical sense of what is likely to make a difference in the classroom. They can advise you on how to help other teachers and administrators see you as a partner, not an adversary.

Decide what your group's goals are. These goals should be specific and measurable, and you should have some idea how to get from here to there.

Focus on one or two goals—for example, that all students be caught up in reading by the end of third grade, that 90 percent of the district's students take and pass algebra by eighth grade, or that two-thirds of the students pass one or more Advanced Placement exams by twelfth grade. (See "Academic Goals for Your Community.")

ACADEMIC GOALS FOR YOUR COMMUNITY

The goals you pick should be ambitious enough that they will lead your school or school district toward excellence. Examples of goals might be:

- All students in the district will be able to read books suitable for their grade level by the end of third grade.[7]
- Ninety percent of students in the district who are academically behind will catch up in no more than three years.
- Ninety percent of the district's students will demonstrate competence in algebra by the end of eighth grade.
- Two-thirds of the district's students will pass one or more Advanced Placement exams by twelfth grade.

These goals should be set working with educators who have high aspirations. They should be ambitious but achievable, based on answering the question: What could our community accomplish together if we did everything right?

Research how far away the district is from meeting the goals. What percentage of students are *not* caught up in reading by the end of third grade? How far are they from being caught up? What percentage of the district's students do *not* take algebra by eighth grade? How many of these are still struggling with algebra in twelfth grade?

Good assessment of student learning is important
If you don't know where the students are, how can you develop
a plan to get them where they need to go? (See chapter 3.)

Identify steps that will help to accomplish the goals and estimate the cost and time required for each step. Goals without a set of steps to accomplish them are just wishes.

Offer to help with the district's planning process. Surprisingly few school districts do goal-based planning. Often they have so many goals that they cannot accomplish any of them, or they do not identify realistic ways to get from here to there.

Although you should do at least as much research as the district's administrators, do not come across as having the attitude that "we know more than you." Listen politely to their views and present your own information in a spirit of helping Be knowledgeable without being a know-it-all.

Work with the school district to identify sources of funding for needed improvements. If taxpayers must be approached for additional funding, be prepared to show that the money will be spent carefully and thoughtfully and that the district investigated and exhausted opportunities to fund the program by reallocating existing funds.

Emphasize your willingness to work in partnership with teachers and administrators. If the schools improve because of a strong community effort, there will be plenty of credit to go around.

CHECKLIST: PARENT INVOLVEMENT

Help your child at home.
☐ Stress learning as Priority Number One.
☐ Provide a stable, secure home environment.
☐ Establish clear rules and routines at home.
☐ Check your child's homework, but don't do it for him.
☐ Show interest in his learning.
☐ Plan after-school supervision for him.
☐ Know his friends and their parents.
☐ Get ideas from teacher on how to help him at home.

Work with your child's school.
☐ Know your child's teachers and principal.
☐ Find out about the school's academic standards.
☐ Know the school's disciplinary policies.
☐ Volunteer at the school.
☐ Stay involved as your children get older.

Learn how schools can encourage parent involvement.
☐ The school clearly welcomes you and other parents.
☐ The school shows interest in your and other parents' opinions.
☐ The staff communicate clearly with parents in language you can understand.
☐ The school provides you with different ways you can help and be involved.
☐ The staff are available during convenient hours.
☐ The school has staff available to speak the language of non-English speaking parents.

Use strategies to overcome barriers to parent involvement.
☐ Focus on results, not methods.
☐ Stress partnership and appreciation for the teachers and other school staff.
☐ Make suggestions for ways you can help.
☐ Ask politely for clear explanations.
☐ Tell teachers what your expectations are for your child.
☐ In case of trouble, follow the chain of command.

CHECKLIST: COMMUNITY SUPPORT FOR SCHOOLS

Get community donations and volunteers for your school.
- ☐ Identify school needs.
- ☐ Identify likely donors.
- ☐ Create a committee to plan, coordinate, and accept contributions.
- ☐ Identify additional resources needed to make good use of contributions and volunteers.
- ☐ Publicly thank contributors and volunteers.

Tie school assistance to specific goals.
- ☐ Know the three types of assistance: general, targeted, and goal based.
- ☐ Establish clear school improvement goals.
- ☐ Identify the resources required to achieve those goals.
- ☐ Show your school improvement plan to donors.
- ☐ Raise money and recruit volunteers to meet the goals.
- ☐ Measure and document your success.
- ☐ Share this information with your school's donors and volunteers.

CHECKLIST: SCHOOL AND DISTRICT PLANNING

Get involved in your school's improvement planning process.

☐ Ask the principal what the school improvement planning process is and how parents can help.

☐ Explain how parent participation can increase parent support.

☐ Identify the school's strengths and weaknesses.

☐ Work with teachers to pick one or two priority areas for improvement.

☐ Follow the principles of good planning: have clear, measurable goals; have well-defined steps to get from here to there; keep track of progress toward the goal.

☐ Listen and read all materials that your committee receives.

Get involved in your school district's improvement planning process.

☐ Combine numbers, persistence, and clear goals.

☐ Include teachers.

☐ Decide on goals and focus on one or two.

☐ Research how far the district is from reaching the goals.

☐ Identify ways to help the district meet the goals.

☐ Offer to help with the district planning process.

☐ Help identify additional sources of funding.

☐ Document results.

NOTES

1. Author's conversation with first-grade teacher Elta Smith, 1988.

2. Chandra Muller, "Parent Involvement and Academic Achievement: An Analysis of Family Resources Available to the Child," in *Parents, Their Children, and Schools*, Barbara Schneider and James S. Coleman, eds. (Boulder, Colo.: Westview Press, 1993), 100–102.

The researcher examined the association between types of parent involvement in middle and high school with grades and standardized test scores. This research uses the 1988 National Education Longitudinal Study (NELS). NELS surveyed parents and students about their home environment and gave students tests developed by the Educational Testing Service to measure reading, math, science, and social studies skills. The study used a statistical technique that makes "apples to apples" comparisons of families with similar incomes and parent education levels.

Higher grades and test scores may result in part from the specific activities mentioned and in part from the overall effect of living in a home with parents who are more involved in their children's education. Music classes emphasize such skills as practice and self-discipline.

3. Meg Sommerfeld, "Ordinary People: The Parents, Teachers, and Community Activists Who Make up Texas Industrial Areas Foundation Show They Can Do Some Extraordinary Things for Schools," *Education Week* (January 25, 1995): 16–21.

The parent who had thought that "the kids were doing fine" mentioned grade inflation as a cause of her misinformation: "At that time, I thought things were fine."If your kid's on the A–B honor roll, then everything must be hunky-dory . . . but we weren't getting the full picture."A second parent commented that "we did not realize the importance of the test score for our kids. . . . It was an eye-opener for us. . . . We realized in this workshop that the report card might tell us one thing, and the test scores tell us another different story about our kids." Richard Murnane and Frank Levy, *Teaching the New Basic Skills* (New York: Simon and Schuster, 1996), 102. See chapter 3 for a discussion of the usefulness of external testing.

4. Interview by Helen Giraitis-Rodgers with Al Mindiz-Melton, January 17, 1997.

5. School planning would seem to be an exception to the "focus on results and not methods" rule: the planning committee must estimate how effective a method is likely to be, over what period of time. However, teachers should still have the primary responsibility for selecting methods. They should be prepared

to explain why they think their approach will work, and parents should receive regular progress reports on the plan's success.

6. Many school districts have a strategic planning process that results in the selection of goals for the district. Find out how you can become a part of this process.

7. Careful exceptions may need to be made for students who just enrolled in the district and for a few severely disabled students. However, the burden should be on the school district to show that those students' disabilities are severe enough to prevent them from learning.

Appendix

Resources for Parents

This appendix contains information on

- general books on education
- books on reading
- books on academic standards
- examples of academic standards
- Internet sites

GENERAL BOOKS ON EDUCATION

The Schools We Need and Why We Don't Have Them, by E. D. Hirsch (New York: Doubleday, 1996). Children benefit from a knowledge-rich curriculum, adult guidance, and early learning to stimulate curiosity, but in some places the trends are in the opposite direction. Why? Hirsch's answers may surprise you.

We Must Take Charge: Our Schools and Our Future, by Chester E. Finn (New York: Macmillan, 1991). Do you know of places where students should be learning more, but all you hear is "The kids are doing fine"? where policymakers focus on teaching methods and dollars spent, but not educational results? where students don't seem motivated to learn? Finn discusses solutions for these problems. His book is an excellent citizen's introduction to education policy.

The Shopping Mall High School, by Arthur Powell, Eleanor Farrar, and David Cohen (Boston: Houghton Mifflin, 1985). If you recognize your local high schools in this book, then your community has a lot of work to do. Shopping malls try to satisfy their customers, and a "shopping mall high school" satisfies the students who don't want to work hard by—you guessed it—not expecting them to work hard. The book shows how this situation can persist without community outrage and how most high schools in the past were probably no better.

Educating for Character: How Our Schools Can Teach Respect and Responsibility, by Thomas Lickona (New York: Bantam Books, 1991). If you're concerned about more than academics, here's the place to start. This book offers practical suggestions on how schools can have a positive influence on students' values, attitudes, and behavior.

231

BOOKS ON READING

Teach Your Child to Read in 100 Easy Lessons, by Siegfried Engelmann, Phyllis Haddox, and Elaine Bruner (New York: Simon and Schuster, 1983). This book has an almost foolproof system for teaching your child to read if she is old enough to pay attention to the lessons.

Teaching Our Children to Read: The Role of Skills in a Comprehensive Reading Program, by Bill Honig (Thousand Oaks, Calif.: Corwin Press, 1996). This book is written for teachers but contains lots of useful information for parents on what your child should learn.

The Read-Aloud Handbook, 4th ed., by Jim Trelease (New York: Penguin Books, 1995). Besides documenting the benefits of reading daily to your children, this book contains a list of good storybooks for children of different ages.

Books to Build On: A Grade-by-Grade Resource Guide for Parents and Teachers, edited by John Holdren and E. D. Hirsch (New York: Doubleday, 1996). What are good books to teach your child about the solar system? about Antarctica? about ancient Rome? about classical literature? This list of books is organized by subject and grade level and is an excellent companion to the *Read-Aloud Handbook.*

BOOKS ON ACADEMIC STANDARDS

What Your Kindergartner [First through Sixth Grader] Needs to Know, edited by E. D. Hirsch (New York: Doubleday, 1996). If you're worried about major gaps in your child's education, this set of seven books (one per grade level) should fill them. The books are based on the Core Knowledge Sequence, a knowledge-rich and user-friendly curriculum.

National Standards in U.S. Education: A Citizen's Guide, by Diane Ravitch (Washington, D.C.: Brookings Institution, 1995). This book is a good introduction to the policy debate on creating national standards.

Geography for Life: National Geography Standards, by Sarah Bednarz et al. (Washington, D.C.: National Geographic Society, 1994). This book shows how interesting and attractive a book of content standards can be. Not surprisingly, it looks a lot like an issue of *National Geographic.*

What Secondary Students Abroad Are Expected to Know, by the American Federation of Teachers (Washington, D.C., 1995). This book compares the U.S. G.E.D. (General Equivalency Diploma) exam with its counterparts in France, Germany, and Scotland.

Making Standards Matter, by the American Federation of Teachers (Washington, D.C., 1996). This publication looks at each state's progress in developing academic standards that teachers can use and parents can understand.

GOOD EXAMPLES OF ACADEMIC STANDARDS

Core Knowledge Sequence (kindergarten through eighth grade)
Core Knowledge Foundation
2012-B Morton Drive
Charlottesville, VA 22903
804-977-7550
Internet address http://www.trinity.edu/departments/education/core/core.html
email address coreknow@www.comet.chu.va.us

Standards of Learning (kindergarten through twelfth grade)
Virginia Department of Education
Division of Technology Production—Attn: Patricia Hicks
P.O. Box 2120
Richmond, VA 23218
804-225-2400
Internet address http://www.pen.k12.va.us/go/Sols/home.shtml

New Standards Project
Elementary, Middle, and High School Standards (three sets)
c/o National Center on Education and the Economy
Publications Department
P. O. Box 10391
Rochester, NY 14610
888-361-6233
Internet address http://www.ncee.org

INTERNET SITES

Achieve
http://www.achieve.org
This organization has played a major role in evaluating state standards and tests.

Advanced Placement Program
Educational Testing Service
http://www.collegeboard.org/ap
This site describes Advanced Placement courses and tests.

Center for Education Reform
http://edreform.com/
Researchers at CER maintain a frequently updated database on state legislation on charter schools, school choice, and other topics.

Core Knowledge Foundation
http://www.coreknowledge.org
This site provides information on the Core Knowledge curriculum, one of the better examples of a clear, high set of academic standards.

Council for Basic Education
http://www.c-b-e.org/
The Council for Basic Education is one of the nation's major school reform organizations promoting high academic standards for all students.

Education Commission of the States
http://www.ecs.org/
This is a good source of information on what different states are doing in education.

Education Policy Analysis Archives
http://olam.ed.asu.edu/epaa/
This site contains scholarly articles on school reform topics.

Fordham Foundation
http://www.edexcellence.net
This site has links to many other education-related sites under the menu item "Suggested Web sites and Resources." Like Achieve, the Fordham Foundation has been a major source of information on the quality of state academic standards.

Great Schools.net
http://www.greatschools.net
This site is a user-friendly guide to help parents choose the best school for their child, track their school's performance, support their children's education, and solve school-related problems. Like the Just for Kids Web site, it is a kind of "Consumer Reports" on schools.

International Baccalaureate Program
http://www.ibo.org
This site describes the academic program that leads to the International Baccalaureate diploma.

Just for the Kids
http://www.just4kids.org
This site has student achievement information on schools in Arkansas, Florida, Minnesota, Tennessee, Texas, Washington, and other participating states. Just for the Kids is a nonprofit data and research organization that compares each school

with the highest-performing comparable schools and investigates promising practices at consistently successful schools.

U.S. Department of Education
http://www.ed.gov
This is another site that is particularly useful for its links to other Web sites.

Glossary

academic failure   Students experience academic failure when they can't do work designed for students of their age or grade level (are *academically delayed*) and do not catch up. Some educators use the term *academic failure* to apply only to cases where the student earns failing grades or drops out of school.

academically delayed   A student is academically delayed if he cannot do work designed for students of his age or grade level. Students who are academically delayed and do not catch up in a reasonable length of time experience *academic failure*.

accelerated instruction   See *remedial courses*.

accountability   Responsibility for results.

accountability system   A set of rules, policies, or practices designed to hold educators accountable, or responsible, for how much students learn. The elements of an accountability system include a description of responsibilities, standards, assessments, reporting of results, and consequences for good or bad results.

advanced courses   Courses that challenge your child. See also *Advanced Placement.*

Advanced Placement   Advanced Placement (AP) tests are designed to assess the student's mastery of first-year college work in a subject, such as French or calculus. Students who receive a 3 or above (on a scale of 1 to 5) can receive college credit for that subject at many universities. These tests are designed and administered by the Educational Testing Service, headquartered in Princeton, New Jersey. Advanced Placement courses are designed to teach the curriculum covered by the AP tests.

anchor papers   See *example papers.*

assessment   An attempt to observe or measure what students have learned.

benchmarks   What students should learn by a specific age or grade level. See also *content standards* and *performance standards.*

ceiling effect   The inability of a too-easy test to show what a student knows—the student can't show her mastery of more difficult material because that material isn't on the test.

charter schools   Public schools that operate under a charter, or contract, with a state or local school district. The rules for charter schools are established by state law and differ from state to state. Some states restrict the number of charter schools that may be established. Usually the charter frees the school from many state and local regulations in exchange for the school's ability to show that its students are successful. For example, a charter school might be able to choose its own books rather than being required to use the state-adopted textbooks.

checklist   A list of skills, attitudes, and/or learning behaviors that students are expected to have.

classroom assessment   Methods the teacher uses in the classroom to keep track of what students have learned, which students need additional help, and which students have mastered the material and are ready to move ahead.

College Board exams   Tests designed to determine readiness to do college-level work.

comparison group   A group of students (also called a *norm group*) who are given a norm-referenced test so that other students' scores may be compared to theirs. The comparison group is supposed to be a representative nation-wide sample of students, so that, if your child does better than 90 percent of the students in the comparison group, you can infer that she would have done better than 90 percent of students nationwide.

constructivism   A belief that the brain processes, organizes, and works to understand all information that it receives. This is sometimes called "constructing knowledge," hence the word *constructivism*. From this, some educators draw sweeping conclusions about teaching methods—for example, that direct instruction should be avoided.

content standards   Descriptions of what students are expected to learn. Examples: "Your child should learn the multiplication table." "Your child should be able to write an essay discussing the causes of World War I." See also *performance standards*.

continuously enrolled   Continuously enrolled students are those who stay in a school over a period of time, as opposed to changing schools.

criterion-referenced test   A test that compares your child's performance with a previously established performance standard. You should receive a report on whether your child did well enough to pass each section of the test. See also *norm-referenced test*.

curriculum   This is sometimes used to mean content standards—what students are expected to know and be able to do. Other times, teachers use the word *curriculum* to refer to methods used to teach students in the classroom. In this book, we use *curriculum* to mean content standards.

developmentally appropriate   This means "appropriate for the student's age and stage." Not all children of the same age are at the same stage—the parent or teacher can judge what's appropriate not by the child's age but by observing his reactions to the activity or material.

direct instruction   A teaching method that emphasizes direct explanation and presentation of information by the teacher. Some direct instruction programs provide a recipe book of proven ways to present the information.

discovery learning   A teaching method that emphasizes students' attempting to solve problems or explain events without being told ahead of time what the "right" solution or method is. For example, children might be asked to guess what might hold the water up in an upside-down jar before being told about air pressure.

dropout rate   The percentage of students entering a grade who drop out within a certain length of time, for example, the percentage of entering ninth-graders who drop out over the next four years. Different ways of calculating dropout rates can yield very different numbers. See the box in chapter 4, "The Dropout Numbers Game."

dyslexia   A learning disability characterized by the student's having difficulty learning to read. Students with dyslexia usually have trouble perceiving separate sounds in words. (See *phonemic awareness*.) Dyslexia must be distinguished from other problems, for instance, ineffective teaching.

example papers   Examples of work, sometimes called anchor papers, representing the school's standards for excellent, good, or satisfactory work at a particular grade level. They are usually anonymous—their purpose is not to honor the authors, but rather to help the public understand what the school's standards are.

exemption   Excusing students from taking districtwide tests. If many students in academic difficulty are exempt from taking the tests, this can artificially raise average test scores. Districts may be able to justify exempting a few severely disabled students.

external assessment   An assessment designed to compare student learning to an outside standard. That standard may be student performance in other schools, a standard for "what students ought to know," or both. Standardized tests are the most common form of external assessment, but not all external assessments are tests. For example, an external assessment might consist of having outside judges grade a student's portfolio or oral presentation using preset standards. See also *on-demand assessment*.

extrinsic motivation   The individual's desire to do something in response to incentives provided by others. These incentives may consist of recognition and social approval as well as money.

first-rate education   A first-rate education enriches your child's life with the best of human knowledge and culture, prepares her to become a responsible, well-informed citizen and to be successful in her chosen occupation, and encourages her to become a lifelong learner.

grade equivalent   An estimate of the grade level at which the average student would score as well as your child did on the test. For example, if your child did as well on a third-grade test as an average entering fourth-grader would, then he has a grade equivalent of 4.0.

grade inflation   The practice of giving high grades to students whose work is not of outstanding quality. Some parents pressure teachers to inflate their children's grades.

"grading on the curve"   Grading students based on their *relative* performances—the top students earn As, the next students earn Bs, and so on, no matter what their actual scores. This can create an incentive for students to pressure their peers not to study.

graduation rate The percentage of students entering a grade who graduate within a certain length of time, for example, the percentage of entering ninth-graders who graduate within four years. Some districts calculate graduation rates only for entering twelfth-graders, after many students with problems have already dropped out.

incentives Rewards or punishments that influence behavior. Some of the most powerful incentives do not involve money. For example, the approval of one's peers is a strong motivator of behavior for teenagers and adults.

individual education plan A plan developed by teachers to get the student up to a standard of learning defined in the plan. Students in special education are required by law to have these plans.

in-school suspension Placing the student in a separate location in the school designated for students who have misbehaved.

intrinsic motivation The individual's inner desire to do something, regardless of what the external incentives are.

Lake Wobegon Effect A situation in which the great majority of states and school districts appear to be above average on norm-referenced standardized tests, because their average students score better than average students in the test's comparison group. A likely cause is that many of the school districts have test score inflation, while test score inflation was less for students in the comparison group.

learning disability A problem with learning resulting not from poor teaching or a mismatch between the teaching method and the individual's learning style, but because the student has a built-in difficulty understanding certain types of information or doing certain types of tasks.

learning styles Different ways in which individuals learn best; for example, auditory learners learn best by listening to information, while visual learners learn better by seeing the same information in pictures or written words.

limited English proficiency Limited ability to speak and understand English. Students classified as limited English proficient may be exempted from taking standardized tests in English.

longitudinal data Information tracking the same students over time. For example, nonlongitudinal data might compare a school's fifth-graders with its third-graders two years ago, even though these are different groups of students. Longitudinal data would keep track of the original group of third-graders as they change schools and grades.

magnet schools Schools that emphasize instruction in particular subjects in order to attract students from across the district who are interested in those subjects. For example, one magnet school may specialize in the fine arts, while another has a strong science program and a third trains students for health-care professions. Magnet schools may also be designed to attract students who are interested in a particular instructional method or philosophy.

manipulatives   Objects that are used to teach math concepts, such as rods of a particular length.

matrix sampling   Administering a long test by dividing the test into parts and giving each student part of the test. This approach provides a better picture of the performance of students as a group than of the skills and knowledge of individual students.

multiple-choice test   A test that requires the student to select one best answer from a set of possible answers printed on the page.

multiple intelligences   Separate abilities in the areas of verbal thinking, mathematical thinking, awareness of how objects fit together in three-dimensional space, musical ability, awareness of other people's thoughts and feelings, awareness of one's own thoughts and feelings, and muscular coordination. Multiple intelligence theory says that "if you're smart in some of these, you're not necessarily smart in the others." A single-intelligence theory would pick a group of abilities for which "if you're smart in some of these, you're probably smart in all of them."

National Assessment of Educational Progress (NAEP)   A testing program designed to measure the educational level of students in the United States. National samples of students in grades 4, 8, and 12 are assessed every few years in reading, writing, mathematics, science, arts, U.S. history, civics, and geography.

norm-referenced test   A test that compares your child's performance with that of a comparison group of students. You should receive a report on your child's percentile rank, or the percentage of test-takers in the comparison group who did worse than your child.

off-level testing   Giving your child a test suitable for the level at which he works, rather than the grade that he's in. For example, a second-grade student doing fourth-grade work in mathematics would take a fourth-grade math test.

on-demand assessment   An assessment where the student responds to questions provided by the tester. On-demand assessments are what we usually think of as "tests." Not all on-demand assessments are given by pencil and paper, for example, a behind-the-wheel driving test.

percentile rank   The percent of students in a comparison group of test-takers who did not do as well as your child.

performance assessment   Assessment that requires the student to do a task that does not involve pencil and paper, such as performing a science experiment, finding information on the Internet, or driving a car. Some educators loosely use *performance assessment* to mean "any assessment that isn't multiple-choice."

performance standards   Descriptions of how well students should learn the material and the quality of work that they are expected to produce. For example, a content standard might say that "the students will learn how to write essays advocating a point of view," while the accompanying performance standard would describe and give examples of excellent, good, and acceptable essays.

phonemic awareness   Sound awareness: the ability to hear separate sounds in words. For example, a child should be able to hear three separate sounds in the word *fish*. (Note that there are four letters but only three sounds.) Also called phonological awareness.

phonics   Teaching children to read unfamiliar words by using knowledge of letter sounds. Good phonics programs teach sound awareness, the ability to hear how sounds blend together to make words. For example, the teacher might show a kindergartener how to read the word *fish* by saying the sounds of the "f," "i," and "sh" and blending them together. Phonics is often contrasted with another teaching approach, whole language, though good teachers use the better ideas from both methods.

phonological awareness   See *phonemic awareness*.

portfolio assessment   Assessment that judges a portfolio (collection) of the student's best work using a set of performance standards. The teacher and/or the student may select the pieces of student work to go in the portfolio.

professional development   Ongoing learning by teachers and administrators. Educators can learn by getting outside training, sharing ideas with their peers, studying research on effective methods, and evaluating their own experiences and performance.

PTO or PTA   Parent-Teacher Organization or Parent-Teacher Association. Many schools have these organizations—their purpose is to assist the school in its mission to educate students. Some PTO/PTAs get involved in assistance targeted to specific goals—for example, they might contribute money and volunteer time to develop a school computer lab or a science resource room with kits and activities that teachers can use for science lessons.

reading level   The student's level of reading proficiency, as measured by a) the difficulty level of the material that she can comfortably read or b) her score on a standardized reading test. The difficulty level of reading material is usually judged by how long and complex the sentences are and how many words they use that are not part of most people's everyday speech.

reliability   Consistency of assessment results: Does the student get the same score when she is tested twice? Does she get the same score when two different teachers grade her paper?

remedial courses   Courses designed to catch students up who have fallen behind. True remedial courses must be distinguished from low-standards courses that don't catch the students up. Sometimes educators make this distinction by calling true remediation "acceleration" or "accelerated courses."

rubrics   Descriptions of student work that earns a particular grade or score. For example, "An A essay has the following characteristics . . ." The purpose of rubrics is to make the school's performance standards clear and to increase the consistency by which student work is assessed.

school choice   Allowing parents to choose the school their child attends without having to move into a specific neighborhood. There are many different school choice arrangements, allowing parents to choose among some or all of the following: magnet schools, charter schools, other public schools in their district, public schools in other districts, or private schools. See also *vouchers*.

school effectiveness   The school's ability to get students to learn. This is evaluated by comparing how similar students do in different schools—the most effective schools are those that can get a particular population of students to learn the most.

sight words   Words that the student must learn to read by memory because they aren't spelled the way they sound. Examples: of, was, one, two, to.

sound awareness   See *phonemic awareness*.

special education   Educational programs for students with learning disabilities or other kinds of handicaps.

standardized test   A test that is designed to be given and scored the same way in different classrooms and schools, to make comparisons across schools possible. Standardized tests may or may not be multiple-choice. See also *external assessment* and *on-demand assessment*.

test score inflation   A situation in which test scores exaggerate what students know.

validity   Whether an assessment measures what it is supposed to: Does the reading test measure how well students can read?

value added   The learning added to what the student already knew at the beginning of the year.

vouchers   A system that would enable parents to spend part or all of their children's share of public school dollars on private school tuition. See also *school choice*.

whole language   Teaching children to read by keeping lots of books and other printed matter around, reading to children and showing them the words, encouraging them to try to read, and encouraging them to write. In addition to this, your child should learn letter sounds, sound awareness, and the ability to sound out words. See also *phonics*.

word families   Words that rhyme and are spelled the same—for example, cat, bat, hat.

work samples   Collections of the student's typical work. These are sometimes distinguished from portfolios, which are usually collections of the student's *best* work.

About the Author

Chrys Dougherty is director of research of Just for the Kids, a non-profit education research organization that presents information to parents and educators on school performance and educational best practice. He is also associate director of the National Center on Educational Accountability, a partnership of Just for the Kids, the University of Texas at Austin, and the Education Commission of the States.

He taught elementary school science and reading in the 1970s and obtained a PhD in Economics from Harvard University in 1992. Prior to coming to Just for the Kids in 1997, he taught economics, statistics, and education policy at the Lyndon B. Johnson School of Public Affairs at the University of Texas at Austin. While at Just for the Kids, he was the editor of *Improving Early Literacy for Preschool Children: A Handbook for Prekindergarten Educators*. He and his wife Mary Ann are parents of two boys, one in elementary school and one in high school.